I0437750

TABLE OF CONTENTS

LIST OF FIGURES

LIST OF TABLES

I. INTRODUCTION

In the wake of the September 11th attacks, elected officials at every level of government pledged to take all steps necessary to protect the American people.[1] The U.S. Congress established the Department of Homeland Security (DHS) and scores of plans and strategies to address terrorism were crafted by local, state and federal agencies.[2] Within the past three years alone, the federal government has created or updated at least seven separate national strategies that relate to combating terrorism and homeland security.[3] The proliferation of counterterrorism strategies and plans and the realignment of responsibilities in the law enforcement and homeland security communities have resulted in role confusion among many local, state, and federal law enforcement agencies.   The uncertainty that exists threatens to undermine U.S. counterterrorism preparedness.   One area where this has been particularly observed is counterterrorism and security planning for major special events.

The Federal Bureau of Investigation (FBI) plays an integral role in all seven of the national strategies, and it has historically played a significant role in counterterrorism and security planning for major special events. The FBI is currently restructuring its mission, traditions, and organizational culture to meet newly articulated goals and objectives.[4] Intelligence, counterintelligence, and counterterrorism have moved to the fore; other traditional FBI roles have been reorganized and reprioritized. Like most government agencies in the post-September 11th world, the FBI is being asked to do more with less. Resource allocation decisions are more critical than ever and these decisions must be enabled by sound strategy.

---

[1] Arnold M. Howitt and Robyn L. Pangi, "Intergovernmental Challenges of Combating Terrorism" in *Countering Terrorism: Dimensions of Preparedness* (Cambridge, Massachusetts, 2003), 37.

[2] U.S. Congress, *Homeland Security Act of 2002.* Public Law 107-296, 6 United States Code 101, November 25, 2002.

[3] U.S. Government Accountability Office, *Combating Terrorism: Evaluation of Selected Characteristics in National Strategies Related to Terrorism*, Open-file report, GAO-04-408T (Washington, D.C., February 2004), 2.

[4] Tanya N. Ballard, "FBI director unveils plan for agency overhaul," *GOVEXEC.com Daily Briefing* (May 29, 2002), http://www.govexec.com/dailyfed/0502/052902tl.htm (Accessed June 11, 2005); and Robert Mueller, Quoted in: "Failure to communicate," by M. Isikoff & D. Klaidman, *Newsweek* (August 4, 2003), 34-36.

This thesis will review background related to major events management and it will identify some of the strategic issues that have emerged in special events since the terrorist attacks of September 11, 2001. It will focus on the subjective and objective components of the systems currently used by DHS and the FBI to categorize and resource special events, and it will evaluate whether the current approach to major event planning is sufficient for contemporary counterterrorism challenges. The thesis will consider how changes in the present system may improve interagency counterterrorism preparedness. Finally, it will apply risk management principles to the interagency special event planning process to determine if these principles are useful for developing a rational, politically defensible, and fiscally responsible approach to federal resource allocation for major special events.

A.   ON STRATEGY

In recent years the boundaries between public, private, and nonprofit sectors have eroded. The United States has moved to a world in which no organization or institution is fully in charge and yet many are involved, affected, or have a partial responsibility to act.[5] The pace of this change quickened after September 11, 2001 and it has dramatically impacted counterterrorism and security planning for major special events. The increased demand for special events planning expertise, the constant tension between requested resources and available resources, and the enormous expense associated with special events management has contributed to a critical need for public and non-profit organizations to think, act, and learn strategically as never before.[6]

Strategy is important because it provides a roadmap for solving complex problems involving organizations, technologies, and resource allocation within a challenging environment.[7] Strategy is derived from the strategic planning process, which Bryson describes as "a disciplined effort to produce fundamental decisions and actions that shape and guide what an organization (or other entity) is, what it does, and why it

---

[5] John M. Bryson, *Strategic Planning for Public and Nonprofit Organizations,* 3rd Edition, (San Francisco, CA, 2004), 6.

[6] Ibid.

[7] Ted G. Lewis, *Critical Infrastructure Protection in Homeland Security: Defending a Networked Nation,* Volume 1 (Monterey, CA, 2004), 4.

does it."[8] A good strategy must have established and tested means by which to apply resources to the attainment of desired objectives or goals. This link between strategy and resources is critical to the FBI special events management program. The manner in which resources are applied is the essence of strategic planning.[9] Goure' goes on to say:

> A good strategy must strive to be efficient. Not only must ends be related to means; they also must be appropriate and relevant to the objective. Strategists speak of the need for a balance between the objectives, the methods employed to pursue the objectives, and the resources available.[10] Strategy must avoid means that demand resources in excess of those available. Conversely, merely because resources are available, they need not be employed. Strategy also must eschew overexpenditure of resources.[11]

Although it would be ideal to write an interagency special events management strategy, the absence of a guiding organizational structure that represents the special events *community* makes such an undertaking difficult. Since applying the process to a network or "community of interest" that crosses organizational boundaries involves so many stakeholders and because implementation has to rely more on consent than authority, the process is likely to be much more time consuming and iterative than strategic planning applied to an organization.[12]

The dynamic nature of homeland security suggests that the identification of strategic issues may be more useful at present than attempting to structure an interagency plan of action. Mintzberg, Ahlstrand and Lampel note: "It is in times of difficult change, when power inevitably gets realigned in unpredictable ways, that political arenas arise... Under these conditions, many things go up for grabs, and people get to feeling particularly insecure. All of this breeds political conflict, especially in strategy making,

---

8 Bryson, 6.

9 Daniel Goure', "Homeland Security," in *Attacking Terrorism: Elements of a Grand Strategy* by Cronin, Audrey Kurth and James M. Ludes, Eds. (Washington, D.C., Georgetown University Press, 2004), 264.

10 H. Richard Yarger, "Towards a Theory of Strategy: Art Lykke and the Army War College Strategy Model," 1997, Cited in Goure', 264.

11 Goure', 264.

12 Bryson, 58.

where the stakes are high."[13] They go on to say that the more significant the strategy and the more decentralized the organization (i.e. the *community* of homeland security), the more likely power relationships are to be accompanied by political maneuvering. This can make it difficult to arrive at a strategy at all.[14]

The focus of this thesis is, therefore, a deliberate strategy that is limited to the FBI special events management program. It is anticipated that the FBI special events strategy may eventually be used as a model for other interagency special event programs. The purpose of this thesis is to identify a way ahead so FBI special event preparedness goals may be expressed "in terms of an 'end state'" towards which the program should strive. This is consistent with the recommendation of the Gilmore Commission in its second report *Towards a National Strategy for Combating Terrorism.*[15] According to the Commission, the idea of an "end state" was critical for three reasons: 1) it would guide resource allocations; 2) it would serve as the basis for establishing accountability; and 3) it would help establish priorities.[16]

Cronin argues that "Crafting a grand strategy against a nonstate threat such as terrorism is challenging; the alternative…is to continue to employ policy instruments in an unbalanced, often contradictory, and even counterproductive manner."[17] She offers three guiding principles towards a grand strategy: integrate, network, and balance. These principles are essential to a successful interagency effort and they will guide the development of the strategy for FBI special events management in the post-September 11th world.

---

[13] Henry Mintzberg, Bruce Ahlstrand, and Joseph Lampel, *Strategy Safari: A Guided Tour Through the Wilds of Strategic Management* (New York, NY, The Free Press, 1998), 240.

[14] Mintzberg, Ahlstrand and Lampel, 241.

[15] Advisory Panel to Assess Domestic Response Capabilities for Terrorism Involving Weapons of Mass Destruction, Second Annual Report, *II. Towards a National Strategy for Combating Terrorism* (Washington, D.C., December 15, 2000), 4-6.

[16] Gilmore II., 4-6 as paraphrased by Daniel Goure', "Homeland Security," in *Attacking Terrorism: Elements of a Grand Strategy*, Cronin, Audrey Kurth and James M. Ludes, Eds. (Washington, D.C.: Georgetown University Press, 2004), 262.

[17] Audrey Kurth Cronin, "Toward an effective grand strategy," in *Attacking Terrorism: Elements of a Grand Strategy.* Cronin, Audrey Kurth and James M. Ludes, Ed., (Washington, D.C., Georgetown University Press, 2004), 265.

B. PROBLEM STATEMENT

This thesis will examine whether the federal homeland security community has effectively organized itself to address the threats facing major special events in the post-September 11th world. The FBI has historically used its unique authorities, responsibilities and capabilities to engage in counterterrorism and security planning for major special events. Since the creation of the Department of Homeland Security, however, counterterrorism planning at special events has become increasingly more complex. Although DHS was established to integrate nearly two dozen federal agencies under unified leadership "so as to function in a complementary fashion, eliminating unnecessary duplication and separating out activities with conflicting missions and goals,"18 DHS efforts related to special events management have resulted in duplication at the federal level that has created confusion within the special events planning community. This confusion may be negatively impacting counterterrorism preparedness.

Statutory and Presidential mandates require that the FBI engage in counterterrorism planning in support of special events. As illustrated by the reports of the Joint Congressional Intelligence Committee; the 9/11 Commission; and the Department of Justice, Office of the Inspector General, the FBI will be held accountable to its responsibilities whether or not it actively embraces or is able to exercise them.19 The goal of this thesis is to articulate a strategy for FBI special events management in the post-September 11th world that is consistent with FBI mandates and responsibilities and that serves as a potential model for the federal interagency special events planning community.

C. METHODOLOGY

The primary research method for this thesis was a content analysis of 1) homeland security literature, government strategies and reports, and observations of experts in the field of special events management, counterterrorism preparedness, and homeland

---

18 George Nesterczuk, "A Successful Start for the Department of Homeland Security Requires Management Flexibility," *The Heritage Foundation, Backgrounder* 1572, July 19, 2002, http://www.heritage.org/Research/HomelandDefense/BG1572.cfm (Accessed June 11, 2005).

19 Thomas H. Kean, Chair, *The 9/11 Commission Report: Final Report of the National Commission on Terrorist Attacks Upon the United States* (New York: W.W. Norton Co., Ltd, 2004); U.S. Department of Justice, Office of the Inspector General, *A Review of the FBI's Handling of Intelligence Information Related to the September 11 Attacks,* (Washington, D.C., November 2004).

security; 2) public sector literature on strategic planning, organizational politics, psychology of terrorism, and risk management; and 3) a qualitative review of source documents related to the DHS and FBI special events management programs.

In addition to the content analysis, the author participated in numerous meetings and briefings related to major events and was actively involved in counterterrorism planning and implementation at recent major special events including the Free Trade Area of the Americas Conference in Miami, Florida in November 2003; the Democratic National Convention in Boston, Massachusetts in July 2004; the Republican National Convention in New York City, New York in August 2004; the Presidential Inaugural in Washington, D.C. in January 2005; the National Football League Super Bowl in Jacksonville, Florida in February 2005; and the International Athletic Association Federation World Track and Field Championships in Helsinki, Finland in August 2005.

The research material was used in a synthesis approach to identify 1) historical background data; 2) emerging strategic issues related to special events management; 3) models for strategic analysis and decision-making; 4) applicable risk perception and risk management principles; and 5) potential areas for corrective action and further research. Because homeland security is a new and emerging discipline, few benchmarks have been established that reflect accepted "community standards." As part of the methodology for this project, the author asked several special events and crisis management professionals from local, state, and federal law enforcement agencies (four), federal homeland security agencies (two) and academia (three) to review and comment on the draft thesis. Many of their comments and observations have been incorporated into the final thesis.

D. SIGNIFICANCE

This thesis will articulate the roles and responsibilities of the FBI so that interagency law enforcement and homeland security partners will understand the FBI's approach to special events management. It is intended to identify a long-term, sustainable, strategic approach for the FBI special events management program that will serve as a model to the interagency special events management community. One expected consequence of this effort is to make the FBI a more effective partner – if not leader – in cooperative planning efforts with other government agencies involved in special events management.

II.   BACKGROUND

The threat of terrorist attack during special events is not new.   At the 1972 Olympic Games in Munich, Germany, Palestinian terrorists attacked the Israeli Olympic team, ultimately killing 11 Israeli athletes.[20]   In the United States, the 1996 Atlanta Olympics were marred by a pipe-bomb explosion that killed one person and injured 110 others.[21] Unfortunately, these incidents are not unique.   Louis Mizell, a former special agent and intelligence officer with the U.S. State Department, has logged 171 terrorist attacks in sport since Munich.[22] Not all attacks have been successful.   Two weeks prior to the 1998 World Cup tournament in France, European police foiled a plot involving over 100 people in seven countries.   Simon Kuper, paraphrasing the book *Terror on the Pitch* by Adam Robinson, wrote that terrorists planned to strike at the England-Tunisia soccer game on June 15, 1998.

> Backed by the former soccer goalkeeper Osama bin Laden, the terrorists planned to infiltrate the Marseilles stadium, shoot some England players, blow up others, and throw grenades into the stands.   Their colleagues were then to burst into the US team's hotel and murder players.   Others were to crash a plane into a nuclear power station near the French town of Poitiers, causing meltdown.   It would have been a European September 11, only worse.[23]

The Olympics and other major special events are considered strategic targets for terrorist groups because these events carry with them tremendous economic and political symbolism.   Special events provide opportunities for terrorist groups to garner international attention, inflict massive casualties, maximize psychological impact, and build coalition support for their cause.[24]

---

[20]Author unknown, *1972 Munich Olympics Tragedy,* http://terrorism.about.com/od/terroristattacksindepth/a/municholympics.htm (Accessed June 11, 2005).

[21] U.S. Government Accountability Office, *Olympic Security: U.S. Support to Athens Games Provides Lessons for Future Olympics,* Open-File Report GAO-05-547 (Washington, D.C., May 2005), 4.

[22] Simon Kuper, "Sport and terrorism are now inseparable" in *Financial Times* (London, England, July 9/July 10, 2005), W21.

[23] Ibid.

[24] William Alfano, U.S. Department of State, *OSAC Threat Overview*, Overseas Security Advisory Council (OSAC) 2006 Security Briefing, U.S. Department of State (Washington, D.C., June 17, 2005).

Incidents that occur at major special events may transcend the event itself. In addition to its effect on participants and spectators, an incident at an international special event may impact diplomacy, politics, business, commerce, finance, or other interdependent realms. This realization led the lead security planner for the 2006 Winter Olympic Games in Torino, Italy to conclude recently, "International cooperation is the most important pillar in securing this type of event."[25]

A.   FBI SPECIAL EVENT PLANNING

In 1996, the FBI created the Special Events Management Unit (SEMU) to centralize the FBI's counterterrorism planning efforts in advance of large-scale special events. According to the 1999 FBI Special Events Management Planning Handbook:

> The threat of deadly violence wherever people congregate for business or pleasure has grown throughout recent years as a result of several phenomena: (1) a mass media capability that allows for worldwide and real-time transmission of pictures and video, (2) an increased tendency for groups and individuals to resort to violence against innocent people in today's asymmetrical world, (3) continued advancements in weapons of mass destruction technology that makes these devices increasingly deadly, and (4) a greater accessibility to these weapons by groups and individuals.[26]

While these threats were very real in 1999, the American public's perception of risk and sensitivity to terrorism did not change appreciably until September 2001.[27] There is now increasing interest in how the United States deals with events where there is considerable ambiguity and uncertainty on the likelihood of their occurrence and their potential consequences.[28] The FBI continues to be presented with opportunities to provide leadership to its law enforcement and homeland security partners through its approach to special events management.

---

[25] Roberto Massucci, Deputy Director, Italian Ministry of the Interior Law Enforcement Office. *The XX Winter Olympic Games Security System*, Overseas Security Advisory Council (OSAC) 2006 Security Briefing, U.S. Department of State (Washington, D.C., June 17, 2005).

[26] U.S. Department of Justice, Federal Bureau of Investigation. *Resource Book*: Special Events Management Planning Handbook (Washington, D.C., 1999), 2-1:1.

[27] Howitt and Pangi, 1.

[28] Howard Kunreuther, *Risk Analysis and Risk Management in an Uncertain World* Paper for Distinguished Achievement Award, Society for Risk Analysis Annual Meeting (Seattle, Washington, December 4, 2001), 3.

B.   SPECIAL EVENTS DEFINED

The FBI defines a *special event* as "A significant domestic or international event, occurrence, circumstance, contest, activity, or meeting, which by virtue of its profile and/or status represents an attractive target for terrorist attack."[29] The FBI has extensive experience in dealing with special events of all magnitude and it has historically split the largest special events into one of three general categories: major sporting events, major political events (a subset of events I refer to as politically charged special events), and National Special Security Events (NSSEs).

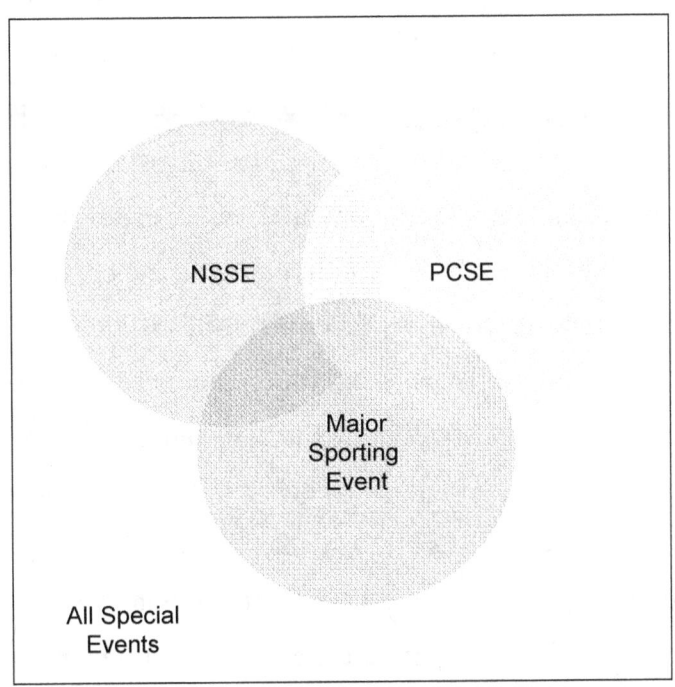

Figure 1.   Three Categories of Special Events

1.   Major Sporting Events

Major sporting events are large-scale sporting contests or games that draw a substantial number of spectators or that generate significant media interest. Examples include the Super Bowl, Major League Baseball All Star Game, the National Collegiate Athletic Association's Final Four Basketball tournament and the Olympic Games. They may have some small political nuance, but they are not generally considered to be

---

[29] U.S. DOJ, FBI, *Special Events Handbook*, 2-1:1.

politically contentious. These types of events represent an attractive terrorist target primarily because of the potential for mass casualties and international media exposure.

2. Politically Charged Special Events (PCSEs)

Politically charged special events, or PCSEs, require a law enforcement response that is different from other special events because PCSEs have wide-reaching political or social impact, and they often occur within a highly-polarized environment. Because of their nature, PCSEs tend to receive extensive media attention; they often draw large numbers of protestors and demonstrators; and they require a significant number of local, state, and federal law enforcement resources. Examples include major political conventions, international trade and economic summits such as the International Monetary Fund/World Bank meetings, and large-scale organized protests and demonstrations. These events represent an attractive terrorist target not only because of the potential for mass casualties and international media exposure, but also because the events themselves have strong symbolic or political significance.

3. National Special Security Events (NSSEs)

National Special Security Events, or NSSEs, are specially-designated events that "have a national significance and could attract unconventional [terrorist] attacks."[30] The Secretary of the Department of Homeland Security (DHS) has lead responsibility for identifying certain events as NSSEs.[31] An interagency federal government working group that is co-chaired by the FBI, the United States Secret Service (USSS), and the DHS/Federal Emergency Management Agency (FEMA) recommends which events warrant NSSE status. This designation does not carry with it any formal funding mechanism or promise for resource augmentation by the federal government, but it does identify those events which the federal government deems to be of major significance. NSSEs may be major sporting events or large-scale PCSEs, but only a small number of special events are designated NSSEs. The 2004 G-8 Summit, the funeral of former President Ronald Reagan, the Democratic National Convention in Boston, Massachusetts, and the Republican National Convention in New York City were all granted NSSE status.

---

[30] President William J. Clinton, *Combating Terrorism: Presidential Decision Directive 62,* (May 22, 1998).

[31] President George W. Bush, *HSPD-7: Critical Infrastructure Identification, Prioritization, and Protection,* (December 17, 2003).

Because of their significance and their potential attraction to terrorists, NSSEs warrant greater federal planning and protection than other special events. Federal law enforcement support for and coordination at these events was mandated by Presidential Decision Directive 62 (PDD-62).[32] PDD-62 provides a framework for federal interagency cooperation through a systematic approach to fighting terrorism and preventing the acquisition and use of Weapons of Mass Destruction (WMD).[33] Much of this organizing framework was reiterated and reaffirmed in the National Response Plan.[34]

For NSSEs, the Department of Homeland Security/United States Secret Service (DHS/USSS) has primary federal responsibility for security design, planning, and implementation; the FBI has primary federal responsibility for law enforcement, intelligence, hostage rescue, counterterrorism, and criminal investigation; and the DHS/Emergency Preparedness and Response Directorate/Federal Emergency Management Agency (DHS/EPR/FEMA) has primary federal responsibility for emergency response and recovery planning and coordination.[35] The guidance provided by PDD-62 and the National Response Plan is very general, and specific planning and resource allocation are left to the individual agencies. The roles and responsibilities of the agencies identified in PDD-62 apply only to events that receive the NSSE designation – a very small subset of all special events. A strategy is needed for organizing the interagency approach to non-NSSEs.

C. FBI AUTHORITIES

Agencies determine the amount and type of support for different special events based in part upon their authorities, responsibilities, and mandates. The traditional federal nexus to special events management is the potential for terrorism – domestic or international. While the potential for terrorism remains the primary connection for federal law enforcement authorities, the FBI also has criminal law enforcement responsibilities that make it a unique partner for state and local agencies charged with policing special events.

---

[32] President Bush, *HSPD-7*.

[33] Ibid.

[34] U.S. Department of Homeland Security. *National Response Plan,* (Washington, D.C., January 6, 2005).

[35] U.S. DHS, *National Response Plan,* 32.

11

Presidential Decision Directive 39 (PDD-39) and PDD-62 identify the FBI as the lead federal agency for terrorism investigations and terrorism-related intelligence collection within the United States.[36] Homeland Security Presidential Directive-5 states that the Attorney General, *usually acting through the FBI*, has lead responsibility for criminal investigations and intelligence activities related to terrorist acts and terrorist threats. HSPD-5 also requires that the FBI coordinate the activities of other members of the law enforcement community to detect, prevent, preempt, and disrupt terrorist attacks against the United States.[37] Additionally, the U.S. Code of Federal Regulations states the FBI shall "exercise lead agency responsibility in investigating all crimes for which it has primary or concurrent jurisdiction and which involve terrorist activities or preparation for terrorist activities."[38] This includes the enforcement of all federal crimes of terrorism, including those occurring outside the United States.[39]

These authorities, and the Attorney General Guidelines, mandate that the FBI be involved in planning for and responding to acts of terrorism. The Attorney General's Guidelines (AG Guidelines) provide clear guidance on how terrorism investigations are to be conducted:

> The FBI shall not hesitate to use any lawful techniques consistent with these Guidelines, even if intrusive, where the intrusiveness is warranted in light of the seriousness of the crime or the strength of the information indicating its commission or potential future commission. This point is to be particularly observed in the investigation of terrorist crimes and in the investigation of enterprises that engage in terrorism. [40]

Effectively policing special events requires strategies that are not limited to the use of terrorism statutes. Specific federal criminal statutes address crimes other than terrorism that may be committed at special events. These include crimes against foreign

---

[36] President William Jefferson Clinton, *Presidential Decision Directive 39,* (June 21, 1995); President Clinton, *PDD-62,* (May 22, 1998).

[37] President George W. Bush, *Homeland Security Presidential Directive 5: Management of Domestic Incidents,* (February 28, 2003).

[38] United States Congress, U.S. Code of Federal Regulations 0.85 (1).

[39] United States Congress, Title 18, U.S. Code, Section 2332b (f) & (g).

[40] U.S. Department of Justice, *The Attorney General's Guidelines on General Crimes, Racketeering Enterprise and Terrorism Enterprise Investigations,* by John Ashcroft (May 30, 2002), 7.

officials, official guests and internationally protected persons;[41] civil disorders and riots;[42] destruction of motor vehicles;[43] solicitation to commit a crime of violence;[44] and interstate travel in aid of racketeering.[45] Under the current AG Guidelines, the FBI is permitted to initiate an investigation "when facts or circumstances reasonably indicate that a federal crime has been, is being, or will be committed."[46] The unique authority of the FBI, when used in concert with the authorities and responsibilities of federal, state and local partners, provide tools for the effective management of potential criminal and terrorist incidents that may occur during special events.

D. INTERNATIONAL SPECIAL EVENTS

Security and crisis planning for international special events is generally the responsibility of the host nation, but the United States government has a vested interest in these events. This was recognized in both PDD-62 and PDD-39, which state, respectively:

> The first duty of government is the protection of its citizens. That duty extends to Americans abroad, whether they are traveling in an official or private capacity. The State Department, through its chiefs of mission, will be responsible...for programs to preserve the safety of private U.S. citizens abroad. U.S. citizens shall be adequately warned of the danger of terrorist attack, advised regarding precautionary measures and afforded appropriate assistance and protection.[47] And;

> It is the policy of the United States to defeat and respond vigorously to all terrorist attacks on our territory and our citizens, or facilities, whether they occur domestically, in international waters or airspace, or on foreign territory.[48]

The FBI assists the State Department with security and crisis management planning and implementation and acts as the lead U.S. investigative agency overseas. For

---

[41] Title 18, U.S.C. Sections 112, 878, 1116, and 1201 (a) (4).

[42] Title 18, U.S.C. Sections 231, 2101.

[43] Title 18, U.S.C. Section 33

[44] Title 18, U.S.C. Section 373

[45] Title 18, U.S.C. Section 1952.

[46] U.S. DOJ, *AG Guidelines on General Crimes, Racketeering Enterprise and Terrorism Enterprise Investigations*, 10.

[47] President Clinton, *PDD-62.*

[48] President Clinton, *PDD-39.*

example, the FBI had crisis management experts and agents prepared to help the Government of Greece process crime scenes and gather evidence in the event of an attack during the 2004 Olympic Summer Games in Athens.[49] Unlike the authorities that outline lanes of responsibility for domestic planning during NSSEs, there are no specific guidelines for U.S. government agencies to follow when planning for an international special event. Based on their experience in Athens, some agency officials at the Department of Defense, Department of Justice, and State Department concluded that further clarification of the agencies' roles and responsibilities in supporting foreign-based events might be helpful, particularly for planning and budgeting resources.[50] A strategy is needed for organizing the interagency approach to international special events.

E. SERL RATING SYSTEM

Prior to the establishment of the Special Events Management Unit (SEMU), no formal process existed to assist FBI planners in determining how FBI resources should be allocated in support of special events. Planners often referred to historic special events cases for general guidance, but few "hard and fast" rules existed that provided a baseline from which planners could construct a tailored special events response. Similar special events were often resourced differently, and the size of the force deployed for a given special event was determined by the political will and influence of the field division's Special Agent in Charge (SAC).

In an attempt to create a more objective way to allocate resources, the FBI created the Special Events Readiness Level (SERL) rating system. The SERL system was an internal FBI classification structure that estimated the attractiveness of the special event as a terrorist target and the amount of FBI resources that would be appropriate to devote to supporting the event. The SERL ratings are numbered one through four, with level four events receiving the least amount of FBI support. The four SERL ratings are defined as follows:

1. SERL I. An event of such magnitude that it warrants the full support of the United States Government (USG). The event will likely necessitate the pre-deployment of USG counterterrorism response assets. The SERL I designation will generally be reserved for a select number of events with

---

[49] GAO, *Olympic Security,* 12.

[50] Ibid.

enormous national or international importance. It requires approval by the Department of Justice acting upon the recommendation of FBIHQ. [An example of a SERL I event is the Olympic Games.]

2. <u>SERL II</u>. Events not of the magnitude of the Olympics, but which may necessitate a limited pre-deployment of USG assets. FBI field offices will usually require an augmentation of their own resources. FBIHQ will often assist the field office with coordinating appropriate assistance from other federal agencies and departments as part of the overall federal response plan. FBIHQ will designate this level of event. [The Presidential Inauguration, national political conventions, and the Super Bowl are examples of previous SERL II events.]

3. <u>SERL III</u>. Those events that require minimal support from other USG agencies/assets, principally tailored to any unique conditions surrounding the event. FBIHQ will normally provide only limited resource augmentation to field offices, with larger offices perhaps requiring none. FBIHQ will designate this level of event, based upon an appropriate recommendation from the affected SAC. [The Major League Baseball All-Star Game and International Monetary Fund/World Bank meetings are examples of SERL III events.]

4. <u>SERL IV</u>. In nearly all instances, these special events are adequately supported by state and local resources. Only minimal support by the FBI field office may be warranted. Other USG agencies may also provide minimal or no support. Unusual circumstances may sometimes necessitate the employment of more resources, but they should be specifically tailored to address the unique needs of the particular event. The affected SAC may designate events as SERL IV and notify FBIHQ of this action. [Games and events of a local or regional nature are examples of SERL IV events.][51]

F. SERL CRITERIA

Eight factors were identified for use in evaluating how much FBI support would be appropriate for a given special event. Although they are not weighted or ranked, the criteria include:

1. <u>Size</u>: This includes the size of both the event and the responsible field office. The greater the number of participants and associated staff, generally the greater the security and safety requirement. Size of the field office is also an important consideration as larger offices may be able to absorb the resource requirements for supporting an event more readily than smaller offices.

---

[51] U.S. DOJ, FBI, Special Events Planning Handbook, 2-5:2.

2. Threat: Relevant considerations include the state of global political affairs, current domestic and global terrorist activity levels, previous acts of terrorism or other violence associated with this event, threats associated with similar events, current threat directed toward this event or attendees, and the realistic degree of danger that known terrorist groups may pose to the event.

3. Significance: Some events have historical, political, and/or symbolic significance that heightens concern about associated terrorist or other criminal activity.

4. Duration: Longer events often require more resources than those of relatively short duration.

5. Location: An event's location may provide an attractive stage for a criminal or terrorist act. Certain locations may require unique capabilities to ensure adequate event security. The geographical dispersion of an event is also an important consideration when determining resource requirements.

6. Attendance: Major events may have a large number of spectators in a relatively confined space, providing an inviting target for various weapons of mass destruction (WMD). Attendees may also include people from disparate cultural, political, and religious backgrounds, some of whom may have antagonistic relationships.

7. Media Coverage: Live media coverage presents terrorists and other criminal elements with a lucrative forum for making a statement to a wide audience. Events with national and/or international media attention, therefore, may provide a more attractive target than those with minimal coverage.

8. Dignitaries: Large events may draw numerous government officials and other dignitaries from around the nation and the world. Domestic and international criminal elements may be attracted to these individuals because of who they are, what they represent, or merely because they are well known.[52]

---

[52] U.S. DOJ, FBI. Special Events Planning Handbook, 2-5:2.

The SERL rating system and criteria established in 1997 are still used by the FBI SEMU. Several strategic issues have emerged since 2001, however, that require the SEMU reevaluate its approach to special events management to ensure it is doing all it can to meet the strategic goal of the FBI to protect the United States from terrorist attack.[53]

---

[53] U.S. Department of Justice, Federal Bureau of Investigation, *Strategic Plan 2004-2009* (Washington, D.C., 2004), 26.

THIS PAGE INTENTIONALLY LEFT BLANK

III. THE EMERGENCE OF STRATEGIC ISSUES

In 2004, the SEMU coordinated FBI counterterrorism efforts in support of more major special events than any previous time in FBI history. Several after-action issues and lessons learned were observed, and a number of priorities were identified. This chapter discusses some of the factors that have contributed to the emergence of important issues that are likely to impact the future of the FBI special events management program. The way the FBI responds to these influences will determine its place in the interagency special events management community.

A. EXTERNAL CHANGES TO THE STATUS QUO

The management of most special events has historically been the responsibility of state and local law enforcement officials. Because of this orientation, special event planning has traditionally been focused on crowd control and public safety. In the past, state and local officials requiring federal government assistance would request law enforcement "crisis management" assistance through the FBI and would request "consequence management" assistance through the Federal Emergency Management Agency (FEMA). Military assistance to civil authorities would generally be coordinated in support of the appropriate Lead Federal Agency (for instance the FBI or FEMA, or in the event of an NSSE, potentially the United States Secret Service (USSS)).[54] Specific federal statutes, Presidential Directives, and interagency plans identified the roles and responsibilities of federal departments and agencies involved in incident management activities.[55] It was assumed and accepted that these same roles and responsibilities applied to planning and implementation activities for major special events. The SERL rating system, originally intended for internal FBI use, evolved to become the "gold standard" that guided the level of support other federal agencies would commit for major special events.

---

[54] U.S. Department of Defense, *Department of Defense Directive 2000.15: Support to Special Events,* (Washington, DC, November 21, 1994).

[55] These interagency plans included the Federal Response Plan and the CONPLAN, both of which have been largely been incorporated into the National Response Plan.

In the post-September 11th world, homeland security policymakers at the federal level have attempted to shift the focus of special events planning away from law enforcement and counterterrorism towards an "all hazards" approach. The terms "crisis management" and "consequence management" have been replaced by the single phrase "domestic incident management."[56] Although the impetus for this may have been to demonstrate that attempts to prevent, protect, mitigate, respond to, and recover from terrorist attacks, major disasters and other emergencies require a single, integrated effort, this change in terminology masks the reality that there are functional distinctions between law enforcement (crisis management) and response and recovery (consequence management) operations that require separate subject matter expertise.

Despite the change in terminology and the shift in focus at the federal level, the primary responsibility for special event planning at the state and local level has remained with law enforcement officials. Local law enforcement officials now need clarification about where to turn for federal assistance for special events – should they continue to look to the FBI for law enforcement leadership or are they expected to forge new special events management partnerships with DHS? Either way, it is incumbent upon the federal government to provide clear guidance and direction.

1.   Accountability and Unity of Effort

In 2002, the Government Accountability Office (GAO) reported that over 40 federal departments and agencies have roles in combating terrorism, and past federal efforts have resulted in a lack of accountability, a lack of a cohesive effort, and duplication of programs.[57] In the time since that report was issued, DHS has created a special events group within their headquarters Integration Staff (I-Staff) and a special events unit within their Information Analysis Directorate. The National Counter Terrorism Center (NCTC) has established a special events unit, and the Department of Defense (DoD) has established a component within U.S. Northern Command that focuses on special events. Additionally, the United States Secret Service (USSS) has increased

---

[56] President Bush, *HSPD-5*.

[57] U.S. Government Accountability Office, *National Preparedness: Integration of Federal, State, Local, and Private Sector Efforts is Critical to an Effective National Strategy for Homeland Security*, Statement of Randall A. Yim, Managing Director, National Preparedness, Open-file Report, GAO-02-621T (Washington, D.C., 2002), 3.

their profile regarding non-NSSE special events and the Bureau of Alcohol, Tobacco and Firearms (ATF) has established a group whose duties include providing support to major special events.

While each of these groups has different responsibilities and authorities, each of them also has limitations on their authorities that preclude them from providing full-spectrum coverage for law enforcement, counterterrorism, intelligence and incident management for major events. Special events management requires consistent national leadership with the authority not only to coordinate the activities of other agencies, but to participate operationally when warranted. In the post-September 11th environment it is less clear which agency or agencies have primacy in coordinating the federal government's response to different special events, and this has resulted in the uncoordinated and sometimes inefficient deployment of federal assets and a lack of effective integration of federal resources.[58]

The role of the DHS is to synthesize the efforts of other departments and agencies to ensure law enforcement operations and response and recovery operations are coordinated. The responsibility to coordinate is different than the responsibility to operate – particularly when new or proposed operations duplicate or confuse existing operations. Although DHS has at least seven operational legacy agencies[59], none of the agencies possess the range of jurisdictional authorities—both criminal and counterterrorism—that are available to the FBI. For example, the United States Secret Service has a great deal of experience in dealing with security related to NSSEs, but it has neither the investigative jurisdiction nor the personnel resources to manage non-NSSEs unless a dignitary under USSS protection is present.

In April 2004, the Secretary of DHS coordinated the development of the Interagency Security Plan (ISP) for the Period of Increased Risk (May 2004-January

---

[58] Several lessons learned regarding the duplication of effort and role confusion have been documented in recent internal and interagency after-action reports. Examples of these reports include the after-action report for the 2004 Republican National Convention and the after-action report for the Washington Nationals Home Opener in Washington, D.C. on April 14, 2005.

[59] Michael Chertoff, *Secretary Michael Chertoff U.S. Department of Homeland Security Second Stage Review Remarks,* (Washington, D.C., July 13, 2005), 6 at http://www.dhs.gov/dhspublic/display?theme=44&content=4597&print=true (Accessed July 14, 2005).

2005).[60]   During the process of developing the ISP, DHS created an internal DHS Special Events Working Group (SEWG) and an interagency SEWG. The interagency SEWG is co-chaired by the DHS Integration Staff (I-Staff), United States Secret Service (USSS), and the FBI.   The Interagency SEWG is composed of headquarters representatives from all federal departments and agencies that have responsibility for or association with special event security and/or incident management. It currently includes representatives from over two-dozen departments and agencies.[61]   Although there is increased interest and participation in the special events planning process, few agencies have realized changes in their authorities or jurisdiction that increase their accountability for special events management. This has increased the complexity of the special events planning process. Every agency now has a voice in the process, but only a handful will be held responsible for the outcome.

The efforts of DHS in establishing the Interagency SEWG and taking a more proactive approach to special events management has been a step toward improving cohesive effort – one of the issues identified by the GAO. Unfortunately, it may have inadvertently resulted in exacerbating another of the problems identified by the GAO – duplication of effort. Following the establishment of the SEWG, the DHS I-Staff created a new rating system for categorizing special events that is nearly identical to the FBI's SERL system. The implementation of this duplicate system for rating special events has resulted in significant confusion among federal, state, and local interagency special events planners.

2.   SEHS Rating System

Derived from several systems in use by other agencies including the USSS, FEMA, ATF, and the FBI, DHS created a four-level Special Events Homeland Security (SEHS) rating system for prioritizing all special events. The four SEHS ratings are defined as follows:

> SEHS–I: Significant Federal assistance and support for situational awareness may be provided to support SEHS-I events designated by DHS.

---

[60] U.S. Department of Homeland Security, *Draft Special Events Homeland Security Standard Operating Procedures,* March 2005, 1.

[61] As the Unit Chief of the FBI Special Events Management Unit, the author serves as the FBI co-chair of the Interagency Special Events Working Group.

Potential areas of assistance include but are not limited to threat and vulnerability assessments; security planning assistance; information management and sharing; intelligence; hostage rescue; counterterrorism; criminal investigation; dignitary protection; medical and health response; medical intelligence assessments; critical infrastructure protection; aviation and maritime security; law enforcement personnel augmentation and coordination; nuclear/radiological security; water safety; hazardous materials; specialized detection equipment (CBRNE—Chemical, Biological, Radiological, Nuclear, Explosive); Explosive Ordnance Detection (EOD); civil disturbance equipment and training; canine resources; specialized military assets; training and exercise support; and other support as required. Pre-deployment of some Federal assets may be warranted in addition to consultation, technical advice or support for a specific functional area in which local agencies may lack expertise or key resources. A Federal Coordinator will be designated and a Special Event Integrated Federal Support plan will be developed for Level I events.

SEHS-II: Selected Federal assistance and support may be provided as required to support SEHS-II events designated by DHS. Potential areas of assistance are similar but to a lesser degree than that of SEHS-I. Limited pre-deployment of Federal assets may be warranted in additional to consultation, technical advice or support for a specific functional area in which local agencies may lack expertise or key resources. A Federal Coordinator will be designated and a Special Event Integrated Federal Support plan will be developed for Level II events.

SEHS-III: Limited Federal assistance and support may be provided for SEHS-III events designated by DHS. Limited Federal support may include consultation, technical advice or support for a specific functional area in which local agencies may lack expertise or key resources. Federal resources will be available to respond as warranted.

SEHS-IV: Special Events designated by DHS as SEHS-IV generally do not meet the criteria warranting direct Federal support and involvement. DHS, through the HSOC and the I-STAFF Incident Management Division, will monitor these events. DHS may assist state and local jurisdictions hosting the event by providing training and exercise opportunities through existing and/or tailored programs, as well as encourage use of existing Federal assistance programs in preparation for such events.[62]

3.   SEHS Criteria

Eleven factors were identified by DHS as important to the SEHS rating system; eight of the eleven criteria are identical to those used by the FBI in its SERL rating

---

[62] U.S. DHS, *Draft Special Events Homeland Security Standard Operating Procedures,* 7-8.

system. The DHS criteria are used for categorizing and designating all special events other than NSSEs. Although not weighted or ranked, the SEHS criteria include:

1. Size: Factors include the size of the event, including multiplicity of jurisdictions involved and the number of participants and associated staff. Larger events are more likely to draw attention of terrorists, or other criminals, seeking to cause mass casualties.

2. Threat: Factors include current threats directed toward this event or attendees; current threats associated with similar events; current levels of domestic and global terrorist activity; previous terrorist incidents or acts of violence associated with the event or similar events; the threat assessment for terrorism and civil disturbance before, during, and after the event; and the state of global political affairs – geopolitical considerations.

3. Significance: The symbolic, political and/or historical significance of the event.

4. Duration: The duration of the event. Events lasting for an extended period of time often require more resources than those of relatively short duration and they potentially provide more opportunities for attack.

5. Location: The location of the event may provide an attractive stage for a criminal or terrorist act. This factor includes assessment of the capability of Federal, state, and local resources available to support the event. If it is a recurring event, local agencies are more experienced. Certain locations may require unique capabilities to ensure adequate event security. The geographical dispersion of an event is also an important consideration when determining resource requirements.

6. Attendance: The number and type of attendees/participants. Major events may have a large number of spectators in a relatively confined space, providing an inviting target for terrorist attacks (i.e. WMD). Attendees may include people from disparate cultural, political, and religious backgrounds, some of whom may have antagonistic relationships.

7. Federal sponsorship or participation: Events with Federal presence may present an attractive target for terrorist acts. Such events are also likely to be high profile and of national significance, therefore also attractive to terrorists. This includes consideration of both the level and complexity of Federal capabilities employed.

8. Media coverage: Focus of national and/or international media attention on the event. Live media coverage presents terrorists and other criminal elements with a lucrative forum for making a statement to a wide audience. Events

with national and/or international media attention may provide a more attractive target than those with minimal coverage.

9. <u>Dignitaries:</u> Participation by high-level U.S. and/or foreign government officials. Large events may draw numerous government officials and other dignitaries from around the nation and the world. Domestic and international criminal elements may be attracted to government officials and dignitaries. The number and rank of the attending officials may affect the assessment of the potential threat and the level of the security deemed necessary.

10. <u>Critical infrastructure:</u> Proximity of critical infrastructure. The number, density, and vulnerability of critical infrastructure sites in proximity to the venue must be considered.

11. <u>State and local capabilities:</u> Size and expertise of state and local police forces, other responders. Adequacy of security capabilities at the state and local level. Adequacy of other state and local resources. Request by state or local agencies for Federal assistance.[63]

In early 2005, DHS created a master list of special events for the United States using the SEHS rating criteria. Known as the *Prioritized List of Special Events*, the list was created based on events information received from federal, state, and local agencies, including the FBI.[64] Many of the events submitted by different agencies for inclusion on the Prioritized List had been previously rated by the FBI using the SERL system. Despite assessing similar characteristics, the readiness levels arrived at using the SEHS system seldom matched the levels designated by the FBI. Consequently, most events now carry two designations, an SEHS rating and a SERL rating. Agencies that previously adopted the SERL rating system to assist them with allocation decisions concerning personnel and financial resources are now faced with choosing between the SEHS designation and the SERL designation when determining the level of support to provide to a given event.

It is important to note that neither the Interagency SEWG nor the DHS I-Staff have authority over the personnel and equipment committed in support of special events. With no real financial "bottom line" at stake, there is no internal restraint built into the SEHS rating system. This creates a paradox wherein subjective political pressure to rate

---

63 U.S. DHS, *Draft Special Events Homeland Security Standard Operating Procedures,* Annex B.

64 U.S. Department of Homeland Security, *Prioritized List of Special Events* (Washington, D.C., April 8, 2005).

a special event at a certain level can overcome the rational and objective attempt to classify the event. This reality, coupled with the lack of a historical reference against which to compare SEHS classifications, results in a tendency for DHS to rate special events at a level higher than the FBI. The absence of a single, objective rating system for guiding resource allocation for major special events would be an important operational issue. The fact that the U.S. government has nearly parallel but often conflicting rating systems elevates this to a strategic issue that must be addressed.

4.   Command and Control

In order to manage incidents of national significance from an "all hazards" perspective, the National Response Plan calls for the Secretary of DHS to appoint a Principal Federal Official (PFO) to be the Secretary's personal representative for any incident of national significance. The NRP states:

> The PFO is personally designated by the Secretary of Homeland Security to facilitate Federal support to the established ICS Unified Command structure and to coordinate overall Federal incident management and assistance activities across the spectrum of prevention, preparedness, response, and recovery. The PFO ensures that incident management efforts are maximized through effective and efficient coordination. The PFO provides a primary point of contact and situational awareness locally for the Secretary of Homeland Security. The Secretary is not restricted to DHS officials when selecting a PFO.[65]

Two additional positions that are defined in the NRP are the Federal Coordinating Officer (FCO) and the Federal Resource Coordinator (FRC). The FCO is the lead DHS/FEMA official designated to coordinate support in the event of Stafford Act emergencies and the FRC is the lead official designated to coordinate response and recovery operations during non-Stafford Act emergencies.[66] In its draft Standard Operating Procedures (SOP) for Special Events, DHS created a new position known as the Federal Coordinator (FC) to serve as the primary, although not exclusive, point of contact for coordinating federal support for designated special events.[67] The FC position is not identified in the NRP or any other interagency policy or procedures document.

---

65 U.S. DHS, *National Response Plan*, 33.

66 U.S. DHS, *National Response Plan*, 34-35.

67 U.S. DHS, Draft *Special Events SOP*, 4.

Despite its similar name, the FC position is functionally different than any of the positions defined in the NRP. The FC position is described as follows:

> The role of the Federal Coordinator (FC) is to facilitate Federal support to the designated Special Event and to coordinate Federal incident management and security assistance activities across the spectrum of prevention, preparedness, response, and recovery, as appropriate. Designated by the Secretary of Homeland Security, the FC serves as the Secretary's representative locally and is the principal Federal point of contact for facilitating coordinated Federal planning and support for SEHS Level I and II events. The FC will normally be appointed from the pre-existing nationwide Principal Federal Official (PFO) cadre.

> The FC must recognize that, although there may be various levels of Federal involvement, most SEHS I & II events are primarily under the jurisdiction of state and local governments. The designated Federal Coordinator is responsible for facilitating coordination of Federal support with the state, local and private sector event planners and participating Federal Departments. In order to assist DHS in maintaining situational awareness of the event, the Federal Coordinator will provide operational and other reports as needed through the Homeland Security Operations Center (HSOC) and the I-STAFF Incident Management Division.

> The FC does not impede or impact the authorities of other Federal officials to coordinate directly with their department or agency chain of command or execute their duties and responsibilities under appropriate laws, orders, or directives.[68]

The authority to establish the FC position was derived from the authority granted to DHS under HSPD-5 to establish a Principal Federal Official (PFO) for domestic incidents.[69] The FC is not the same as a PFO, however, and any non-NSSE special event would generally not be considered a domestic "incident" unless something significant were to occur at the event. No specific legislation, executive order, or interagency agreement formally codifies the position of the FC, and consequently the position carries with it no authority to command, control, or coordinate the efforts of different federal agencies.

---

68 U.S. Department of Homeland Security, *Integrated Federal Support Plan for Major League Baseball 76th All-Star Game July 12, 2005,* Detroit, Michigan (Washington, D.C., June 2005), 3.

69 Robert Shea, Director of the DHS Integration Staff, personal interview by the author, Washington, D.C., May 6, 2005.

The theory of having a single federal point of contact seems sound, but the creation of the FC in the absence of any formal authority or interagency consensus obscures accountability and results in duplication of effort. The Homeland Security Act of 2002 grants some authority to the Secretary of DHS to establish positions to help him manage the Department, but this flexibility does not tolerate confliction with other formal authorities such as legal statutes or presidential directives. In fact, the creation of the FC position may be in conflict with HSPD-5.

As stated previously, HSPD-5 reaffirms the authority of the Attorney General, usually acting through the FBI, to coordinate the activities of other members of the law enforcement community to detect, prevent, preempt, and disrupt terrorist attacks against the United States.[70] Because the responsibility for special event planning at the state and local level continues to fall to law enforcement officials, and because the primary interest of federal special events planners is law enforcement and counterterrorism, the FBI has the lead responsibility for coordinating law enforcement special events planning efforts.

The fact that the FC may be appointed from the "pre-existing nationwide Principal Federal Official cadre"[71] is another potential concern for state, local, and federal interagency special event planners. This policy makes it possible for the primary, although not exclusive, point of contact for the coordination of federal assets to be an executive from the Department of State, Environmental Protection Agency, Transportation Security Administration, U.S. Marshals Service, or other agency whose core mandates and jurisdiction may not involve special event counterterrorism planning or response. In two recent events, the Federal Coordinators were law enforcement executives from non-DHS agencies that typically play a supporting role in domestic terrorist incidents and special events.[72] Under these circumstances, it is easy to

---

[70] President Bush, *HSPD-5*.

[71] U.S. DHS, *Integrated Federal Support Plan*, 3.

[72] In June 2005, an executive from the Department of State's Diplomatic Security Service was appointed the Federal Coordinator for the Organization of American States meeting in Miami, Florida. In June 2005, an executive from the Department of Justice's Bureau of Alcohol, Tobacco, and Firearms was appointed the Federal Coordinator for the NBA Finals Series games in Detroit, Michigan.

understand how state and local law enforcement agencies could be confused about which federal agency is responsible for coordinating law enforcement efforts for major special events.

B.   INTERNAL CHANGES TO THE STATUS QUO

The FBI SEMU was originally conceived to manage preparedness activities for major events such as the Olympics, World Cup soccer, and the Presidential Inauguration but its mission has expanded dramatically since the terrorist attacks of September 11, 2001. With this expansion, the costs related to special events management have become much more apparent.

1.   Mission Expansion

Any large gathering of people is now *presumed* to be an attractive target for terrorist attack, and FBI field divisions have responded by opening cases on special events that previously would not have merited the attention of federal law enforcement officials. Fueled in part by the fear of potential terrorist attack and in part by public and political pressure to demonstrate preparedness, FBI field divisions are increasingly requesting the services of FBI national assets to assist with operational response planning and implementation for special events of all size, scope, and duration. The following table illustrates the number of FBI special events cases from fiscal year 2000 through fiscal year 2005.

Fiscal Year	NSSE Events	SERL I Events	SERL II Events	SERL III Events	SERL IV Events	Total Events
2000	6	0	0	0	86	86
2001	1	0	2	8	99	109
2002	4	1	3	18	184	206
2003	0	0	3	40	273	316
2004	5	1	4	58	317	380
2005	2	0	3	54	315	372

Table 1.   FBI Special Event Cases 2000-2005[73]

2.   The "Cost of Doing Business"

Since 2001, unprecedented security measures have been implemented or upgraded throughout the United States and the federal government has spent billions of dollars on prevention, preparedness and response programs.[74] In the haste to secure the homeland, however, the U.S. may have inadvertently played into the hands of its enemies. According to Michael Scheur (Anonymous), the United States may have entered into a period of "quiet, steady, unnoticed bleeding:"[75]

> The 11 September attacks, of course, devastated the U.S. economy; it is only now, in early 2004, recovering. But beyond the immediate impact lie massive expenditures – at all levels of American government – that will add permanently to the size and cost of government. In addition to the cost of hiring thousands of federal employees for homeland security purposes; acquiring buildings, equipment, and training to make them effective; and requiring proportionate upgrading at state, municipal, and local levels; there lie what must be substantial amounts of unpredictable expenditures for overtime wages – in government and business alike –

---

[73] FBI Special Events Management Unit, July 5, 2005. The figures for fiscal year 2005 reflect only ten months' activity (October 1, 2004 – August 1, 2005). NSSEs are also given a SERL rating, so the number of NSSEs was not used in the computation of total events.

[74] President George W. Bush, *Securing the Homeland, Strengthening the Nation,* (Washington, D.C., 2002), 31-37.

[75] Michael Scheur (Anonymous), *Imperial Hubris: Why the West is Losing the War on Terror,* (Dulles, Virginia, 2004), 100.

whenever Washington raises the threat level, or when high levels of security are provided at public places or functions heretofore not seen as serious security risks.[76]

The economic drain is not limited to the homeland security buildup. In an attempt to fight the "war on terror,"[77] the United States has adopted a policy of pursuing terrorists wherever they may be – whether at home or abroad. Preemptive warfare imposes its own set of economic costs that threaten to hasten the loss of American primacy.[78] Steven Biddle cautions, "Since 2001, the government has systematically failed to provide revenues sufficient to cover its costs....Barring major changes in American fiscal policy, large, sustained expenditures for ongoing preemptive warfare can be expected to create corresponding increases in federal budget deficits."[79] The financing for these deficits now comes predominantly from foreign lenders. This transfers capital, and thus productive resources, from America to other great powers, contributing to further economic decline.[80]

The economic impact of securing special events was most recently illustrated in 2004 and 2005 when the FBI and its interagency partners engaged in counterterrorism preparedness and security planning for an unprecedented seven NSSEs within a 13-month period. Two State of the Union Addresses, the Group of Eight (G-8) Summit, the funeral for Former President Ronald Reagan, the Democratic and Republican National Conventions, and the Presidential Inaugural resulted in the expenditure of millions of dollars on preparedness activities. The Presidential Inaugural alone was estimated to cost the U.S. and District of Columbia governments over $40 million.[81]

The expenses related to the deployment of FBI national assets are borne by the FBIHQ Counterterrorism Division, and resources expended in the management of special

---

[76] Scheur, 102.

[77] President George W. Bush, Address to Joint Session of Congress, September 20, 2001.

[78] Steven D. Biddle, *American Grand Strategy After 9/11: An Assessment*, Monograph for the Strategic Studies Institute, U.S. Army War College, ISBN 1-58487-188-1 (Carlisle, Pennsylvania, 2005), 17-18, located at http://www.carlisle.army.mil/ssi/pubs/display.cfm?PubID=603 (Accessed June 6, 2005).

[79] Ibid.

[80] Ibid.

[81] Timothy Dwyer, "Tight Security, Strong Opinions Dominate a Day Full of Divisions," *Washington Post*, (Washington, D.C., January 21, 2005), A1.

events represent *opportunity costs* that are not available for other national counterterrorism or crime-fighting initiatives. The table on the following page illustrates the actual FBIHQ Counterterrorism Division costs related to recent special events. The figures reflect the cost of travel, equipment, lease of space, Joint Operations Center upgrades, etc., but do not reflect the direct costs borne by the supporting FBI field divisions or any indirect costs such as salaries or benefits of employees and contractors.

Event	Employees on Temporary Duty Travel	Cost
Super Bowl XXXVIII Houston, TX (2004)	66	$172,355.00
Super Bowl XXXIX Jacksonville, FL (2005)	191	$640,161.00
Major League All Star Game Houston, TX (2004)	6	$6,000.00
Major League All Star Game* Detroit, MI (2005)	48	~$76,407.00
G-8 Summit Sea Island, GA (2004)	865	$2,875,685.00
Republican National Convention New York City, NY (2004)	62	$264,000.00
Democratic National Convention Boston, MA (2004)	104	$482,831.00
Summer Olympic Games Athens, Greece (2004)	123	$3,025,241.00
Total	**1465**	**$7,542,680.00**

Table 2.   FBI Major Special Events Costs 2004-2005. [82]

The increased demand for special events planning expertise, the constant tension between requested resources and available resources, and the enormous expense associated with special events management has contributed to a critical need for the FBI to reevaluate the way it manages special events. In short, the need exists for the FBI to adopt a more strategic approach to managing special events.

---

[82] FBI Special Events Management Unit, July 5, 2005.

IV.   TOWARDS A STRATEGIC APPROACH

The emergence of unique challenges and new strategic issues requires a realignment of FBI strategy.   In order to respond effectively to changes in their environments, public and non-profit organizations must understand the external and internal contexts within which they find themselves.[83] One way to accomplish this is to conduct an analysis that addresses the strengths, weaknesses, opportunities, and challenges facing an organization.[84]

A.   SWOC ANALYSIS

A strengths, weaknesses, opportunities, and challenges (SWOC) analysis of the FBI's SEMU was conducted to identify the external and internal issues related to the FBI's special events management program. This analysis was conducted as a part of an overall reevaluation of the FBI's approach to special events management in the post-9/11 world. It was anticipated that by identifying strategic issues facing the FBI, similar issues would be identified within the greater special events management community. Consistent with the framework identified by Bryson, four questions were addressed during the SWOC analysis.[85] The questions addressed during the SWOC analysis are listed below:

> What major external or future opportunities are available to the FBI?
> What major external or future challenges are facing the FBI?
> What are the FBI's major internal or present strengths?
> What are the FBI's major internal or present weaknesses?

The full results of the SWOC analysis are listed in Appendix A. Bryson divides the issues facing organizations into two broad categories: strategic issues and operational issues.   "Generally, strategic issues imply a need for exploring or creating new knowledge, whereas operational issues imply exploiting existing knowledge."[86] From the list generated during the SWOC analysis, several strategic issues emerged:

- The FBI has long been involved in the process of planning for and managing special events. Major sports contests, political conventions,

---

83 Bryson, 123.

84 Ibid., 125.

85 Ibid., 141.

86 Bryson, 155.

large-scale demonstrations, and other high-profile events have historically involved logistics planning and interagency coordination. There are now more participants and seemingly less clarity about who does what – what is the appropriate way ahead?

- The FBI's Special Event Readiness Level system provides guidance for the amount of support to be provided to special events that are managed by FBI field offices. How valid are the eight criteria that have been historically used to evaluate special events and to set the SERL rating? Do these criteria need further definition now that there are more players in the process? Can the FBI criteria be reconciled with the DHS criteria for a single interagency rating system for all special events?

- The FBI must find a more effective way to manage special events and to handle counterterrorism preparedness. This can/should be done under a single strategic plan that is both 1) rational, and 2) politically defensible. This will require an analysis of objective and subjective factors that influence the management of special events. It is expected that models will need to be developed and evaluated in terms of risk management and cost-effectiveness.

- FBI and interagency partners need to integrate services rather than replicate them. How can the FBI integrate its assets and resources with interagency partners to support counterterrorism efforts at special events in a coordinated, comprehensive, and fiscally responsible way?

B. SYSTEMS ANALYSIS

Resolution of these issues requires an understanding of the objective and subjective components of the system currently used by the FBI to manage special events. This *systems analysis* approach will help to frame the complex issues in a way so they can be modeled and more fully understood.[87] This will allow the FBI to identify possible ways to improve the approach to special events management and it will contribute to a more systematic process for making resource allocation decisions.

1. Objective Factors

Objective analysis is a deliberation made from a less than personal or neutral viewpoint.[88] It uses scientific, often quantitative, methods to measure the likelihood of a threat or incident and to identify known threats, vulnerabilities, and risks. Each special event is unique, and most are influenced by innumerable variables that are not easily quantified. For these reasons, purely objective analysis in the field of special events

---

[87] Bryson., 46.

[88] Wikipedia, *The Free Encyclopedia*, at http://en.wikipedia.org/wiki/Objective_analysis (Accessed June 18, 2005).

management is impossible. A type of objective analysis that may be useful for special events planners is the "empirical research" methodology used by courts to determine if psychological treatments are considered to be legitimate. This methodology requires evidence of conventional use by peers, evidence of use by a "significant minority" of practitioners, and evidence of cost effectiveness.[89]

As noted previously, the FBI developed the SERL system in an attempt to create an objective way to allocate resources for major special events. In the context within which the SERL system was developed, it can be considered a somewhat objective analysis. Consideration is given to certain criteria and, based on the results of the analysis an event is given a readiness level. This approach was appropriate for the number of events worked by the FBI prior to September 11, 2001 because there was generally consensus about what constituted a major special event and what counterterrorism assets and capabilities would be required to support a significant event. The system was adopted and used by a number of federal agencies involved in special events planning, and it allowed the agencies to determine relative resource levels for different level events. The SERL system worked as it was intended, and it was as objective as it needed to be. The current system may no longer be effective.

As the number of special events managed by the FBI has increased, the distinctions between resource levels have blurred and there are few clear benchmarks against which to measure different resource needs within a given SERL. The eight SERL criteria have long been defined, but they are not weighted or ranked and no subordinate criteria have been identified or developed to help planners determine SERL ratings for new or unique special events. For instance, when an event is rated based on "size," there is no direct correlation between the number of participants in an event and its SERL rating. If the analysis were to be truly objective, thresholds would be established that would ensure that as the number of participants increased, consideration would be given to increasing the SERL rating. Establishment of a matrix that would break each of the eight criteria into threshold levels would be a good first step toward improving objective

---

[89] Dr. Larry Beutler, *Psychology of Fear Management and Terrorism*, Lecture at the Naval Postgraduate School (Monterey, CA, April 12, 2005).

analysis and informing the resource allocation decision-making process. A potential starting point for development of this matrix is offered at Appendix B.

2. Subjective Factors

Subjective analysis refers to a deliberation where the feelings of the individuals taking part determine the outcome.[90] It uses judgment, experience, intuition, and other qualitative methods to identify possibilities related to threats, vulnerabilities, and risks. Subjective analysis may include interpretation or bias, but it is necessary for the synthesis and integration of information. Subjective analysis equates to what psychologists call the "clinical wisdom" approach to mental health treatment. Many treatments are assumed to work because of the experiences of those who use them. What is important in this approach is how long someone has used a particular treatment program, how many times they have used it, and the concrete examples they provide as to how it worked. Decisions are made based on clinical experience, good intentions, and "reasonable theory."[91]

Subjective analysis is the dominant approach to special events management in the FBI. The structure of the current special events management program presumes that sufficient expertise exists both in the field and at FBI Headquarters (FBIHQ) to ensure that events are resourced appropriately. Staffing shortfalls and the reallocation of personnel to more critical counterterrorism programs have combined to make this approach unreliable. Experience with event planning, crisis management, major investigations and tactical operations is critical in determining the resources required to manage any given event. This experience varies from one office to the next. Large field offices such as New York and Washington are accustomed to managing large groups of people and significant special events. Small field offices may have very limited experience with special events. Ironically, the subjectivity in the current system may result in large offices under-reacting to certain special events and may result in these offices being caught unprepared. Small offices on the other hand may over-react to events and may misapply critical financial and personnel resources. Neither approach is efficient or effective.

---

90 Wikipedia, *The Free Encyclopedia*, at http://en.wikipedia.org/wiki/Subjective_analysis (Accessed June 18, 2005).

91 Beutler.

Woo argues that the use of expert judgment (subjectivity) is not a very reliable approach and that an underlying structural event model is needed. He concludes "It is hard to avoid a fair measure of expert judgment in terrorism risk assessment, but minimizing subjectivity is key to the scientific evolution of terrorism risk modeling."[92]

3.   Other Factors

The FBI's approach to crisis management and special event planning presumes a three-tiered national response. A *Tier I* response is the responsibility of the local field division. A *Tier II* response occurs when the incident or event exceeds the capability of a single office or it becomes protracted and there is a need for relief teams from neighboring offices. A *Tier III* response is a full national response involving specialized national assets. The level of response is dictated by the FBI's on-scene commander, with concurrence from FBIHQ.

The three-tiered response system is effective for managing critical incidents and major FBI investigations, but this structure is not sufficient to support the planning that is required for special events. Although some responders to a given critical incident may be selected based on knowledge and experience, the overall tiered response structure is based on geography. Not all field divisions or regions have similar experience in dealing with the national plans and policies that impact major special event planning, and no detailed template exists that guides field managers through the nuances of the special event planning process. Consequently, field-based planners may call for regional resources when they are not necessarily warranted, or they may avoid calling for pre-positioned assets until it is too late to manage the logistics associated with their deployment. This negatively impacts consistency in the national special events management program, and fails to capitalize on the experience and expertise of headquarters-based special events program managers.

Even within FBI headquarters divisions, however, there is some inconsistency in the special events program. The FBI has separate headquarters units in disparate divisions that have responsibility for planning for special events and critical incidents. The SEMU is managed under the Counterterrorism (CT) program at FBI Headquarters

---

92 Dr. Gordon Woo, *The Evolution of Terrorism Risk Modeling*, Submitted for the Journal of Reinsurance (London, England, April 22, 2003), 3.

and its planning efforts have historically been focused on deploying and staging assets for counterterrorism response. The SEMU coordinates the administration and logistics related to the deployment of crisis managers, tactical personnel, explosives and hazardous materials specialists, and intelligence analysts, but field division personnel generally determine how to use the specialty assets.

The Crisis Management Unit (CMU) within the Critical Incident Response Group (CIRG) primarily conducts planning for critical incidents, but it also has some responsibility for special event planning. CIRG is an operational FBI headquarters division based in Quantico, Virginia that manages most of the FBI specialty assets that are deployed to assist with major special events and other incidents of national significance. CIRG assets are employed to assist with critical incidents and major investigations under both the counterterrorism and criminal investigative programs. CMU has significant experience with high-profile criminal cases, interagency command post operations, case information management, and operational integration of local, state, and federal resources during critical incidents. Co-locating these planning operations would improve consistency, increase accountability and reduce duplication of effort.

C. REALITY CHECK

The FBI currently uses a combination of objective and subjective factors to determine how to resource major special events, but the approach is disproportionately subjective. As the reports of the Joint Congressional Intelligence Committee, the 9/11 Commission, and the Department of Justice Office of the Inspector General illustrate, another terrorist attack will be reviewed with intense scrutiny.[93] Questions will inevitably come about how counterterrorism planning was conducted and how resource-allocation decisions were made. If the FBI is to create a rational, politically defensible and fiscally responsible approach to resource allocation for special events, it should consider restructuring the special events program to make it more effective. This will demonstrate that the FBI takes its counterterrorism preparedness responsibilities seriously, and that it has the flexibility and adaptability required for success in the post-

---

[93] Thomas H. Kean, Chair, *The 9/11 Commission Report: Final Report of the National Commission on Terrorist Attacks Upon the United States* (New York, W.W. Norton Co., Ltd, 2004); U.S. Department of Justice, Office of the Inspector General, *A Review of the FBI's Handling of Intelligence Information Related to the September 11 Attacks* (Washington, D.C., November 2004).

9/11 world. Finally, reorganization of the FBI's SEMU to address its strategic issues could serve as a catalyst for change in the wider special events management community. This contribution would have a lasting impact on homeland security.

THIS PAGE INTENTIONALLY LEFT BLANK

V. EXPLORATION OF DECISION-MAKING MODELS

An initial objective of this project was to explore whether an objective decision-making model such as Model-Based Vulnerability Analysis (MBVA) could be used to identify a more systematic way to allocate resources for special events. Designed for achieving critical infrastructure protection under budgetary constraints, MBVA is a comprehensive method of analysis that combines network, fault, event, and risk analysis into a single methodology for quantitatively analyzing a sector component such as a hub.[94] MBVA is a scientific, rational approach that would provide an empirical basis for resource allocation decisions. It was hoped that MBVA would be able to predict the consequences of alternatives, provide a means for cost analysis, and contribute to the development of measures of effectiveness and risk. Finally, it was hoped MBVA would provide an objective basis for communicating critical trade-offs and to articulate ways to manage the risk and uncertainty that surrounds special events.

A. RATIONAL PLANNING MODEL

It quickly became apparent that MBVA would not be the best decision-making model for special events management. Consistent with what Bryson calls the *rational planning model*, MBVA favors the use of quantifiable, objective criteria to assist with resource allocation decisions. The rational-deductive approach to decision making begins with goals; policies, programs, and actions are then deduced to achieve these goals.[95] The rational model is a fundamental social science model for how human beings behave. It requires certain assumptions, including the following:[96]

- Human beings have objectives and they organize everything they do to achieve those objectives. They weigh costs/benefits logically to determine if their actions will achieve stated objectives.

- People know the alternatives and know they have choices.

- People understand the consequences of their choices.

- People can assess the probability of the outcomes based upon their actions.

---

[94] Lewis, Chapter 5, 2.

[95] Bryson, 17-18.

[96] David Tucker, *Asymmetric Warfare and Homeland Security,* Lecture at the Naval Postgraduate School (Monterey, CA, June 17, 2004).

This model may not be flexible enough to account for the complex network of relationships that must be developed during the special event planning process. Bryson notes that a fundamental assumption of the rational model is that either there will be a consensus on goals, policies, programs, and actions necessary to achieve organizational aims or there will be someone with enough *power and authority* that consensus does not matter.[97] Planning for special events requires the identification of numerous stakeholders, identification of issues of import to those stakeholders and the development of personal relationships to resolve the issues as planning moves forward.

Event planning requires a networked rather than hierarchical structure, and complex interdependencies are often infused with emotions, politics, and power.[98] Consensus must be built – it cannot be demanded or rationalized through the use of probability and statistics. Woo argues:

> The most rigorous attitude to any risk model development spurns the excessive use of expert judgment, and terrorism risk is no exception. The use of expert judgment can be minimized through exploring and developing mathematical models and simulations of the underlying causative processes, which can then be parameterized from observational data.[99]

This type of approach is not likely to receive the endorsement of police, firefighters, paramedics, and emergency managers because they recognize the value of flexibility and adaptability in problem solving.

B. POLITICAL PLANNING MODEL

Special event planning has a *political* decision-making component that cannot be captured in the rational planning model. Almost all imaginable organizations, private as well as public, are at least mildly or occasionally political.[100] Any decision-making approach that does not acknowledge politics and power assumes that senior managers are rational actors who define strategies that everyone else embraces, compliant and loyal "labor inputs" that they are.[101] We know this is not true in most organizations, and it is

---

[97] Bryson, 18.

[98] Mintzberg, Ahlstrand, and Lampel, 235.

[99] Woo, 3.

[100] Mintzberg, Ahlstrand, and Lampel, 240.

[101] Ibid., 236.

certainly not true in collaborative organizational politics. Public servants are not mere "robots" who implement the strategies that spring "fully armed from the forehead of an omniscient policymaker."[102] The politics and power school of strategic management is consistent with Bryson's *political decision-making model.* This model is inductive, not deductive. It begins with issues, which almost by definition involve conflict, not consensus.[103] Bohlman and Deal have set out the following propositions about the world of organizational politics.

1. Organizations are *coalitions* of various individuals and interest groups.

2. There are *enduring differences* among coalition members in values, beliefs, information, interests, and perceptions of reality.

3. Most important decisions involve the allocation of *scarce resources*—who gets what.

4. Scarce resources and enduring differences give *conflict* a central role in organizational dynamics and make *power* the most importance resource.

5. Goals and decisions emerge from *bargaining, negotiation,* and *jockeying for position* among different stakeholders (original emphasis included).[104]

In special events management, issues are often resolved through the implementation of various policies and programs that serve as treaties that represent a reasonable level of agreement among the various stakeholder groups. Various actors and coalitions of actors pursue their own interests and agendas, and special events managers must maneuver through a complex world of human relationships wherein people must put aside their personal differences to focus on the desired outcome. Subjectivity and the influence of political nuance are an inescapable reality of the landscape of special events management.

C. A HYBRID APPROACH

The ideal strategic planning model for special events must therefore be a hybrid that includes components of both the rational decision-making and political decision-making models. The successful model must take into account objective and subjective factors in a comprehensive, integrated *systems* approach. The use of objective tools will

---

[102] Mintzberg, Ahlstrand, and Lampel, 240.

[103] Bryson, 18.

[104] L.G. Bolman and T. E. Deal, *Reframing Organizations: Artistry, Choice, and Leadership*, Second Ed., (San Francisco, CA: Jossey-Bass, 1997), cited in Mintzberg, Ahlstrand, and Lampel, 239.

ensure that the model can be logically defended, replicated, and applied consistently across different types of special events. The use of subjective tools based upon common assumptions agreed upon by key stakeholders will ensure that those elements most prone to subjective interpretation are viewed as starting points for negotiation rather than unyielding end-states. The hybrid approach allows special events planners to *control* the influence of subjective factors (such as undue political pressure) rather than engage in the futile pursuit of attempting to *eliminate* them. This is the essence of balance – one of Cronin's three guiding principles for a grand strategy.

VI.   THE APPLICATION OF RISK MANAGEMENT PRINCIPLES

The practice of Homeland Security requires the application of information and insight from a number of different disciplines to a new set of problems. It is anticipated that by linking an understanding of risk perception with the tools of risk assessment, the FBI may be able to develop risk management options that are likely to be successfully implemented in the management of special events.[105] A risk assessment methodology can support a homeland security strategy that prioritizes responses to threats, including investments of resources on the basis of both the likelihood of an event and the consequences should one occur.[106]

The 9/11 Commission recommended that homeland security assistance should be based on an assessment of risks and vulnerabilities.[107] *The National Strategy for Homeland Security* states, "…we must carefully weigh the benefit of each homeland security endeavor and only allocate resources where the benefit of reducing risk is worth the amount of additional cost."[108] The most effective way to apply a risk-based approach is by using the trio of threat, vulnerability and consequence as a general model for assessing risk and deciding on the protective measures we undertake.[109] These guiding principles will be the basis for discussion in this chapter.

A.   THREE FUNDAMENTAL VIEWS OF RISK

Risk in the modern world is confronted and dealt with in three fundamental ways. *Risk as feelings* refers to our fast, instinctive, and intuitive reactions to danger. *Risk as analysis* brings logic, reason, and scientific deliberation to bear on hazard management. When our ancient

---

105 Kunreuther, *Risk Analysis and Risk Management in an Uncertain World,* 3.

106 Raymond Decker, "Homeland Security: Key Elements of a Risk Management Approach," testimony before U.S. House of Representatives Committee on Government Reform Subcommittee on National Security, Veterans Affairs and International Relations, *Combating Terrorism: Assessing the Threat of a Biological Weapons Attack,* 107th Cong., 1st Sess., October 12, 2001.

107 Kean, *The 9/11 Commission Report,* 396.

108 Bush, *The National Strategy for Homeland Security,* 64.

109 Michael Chertoff, *Remarks at George Washington University,* March 16, 2005.

instincts and our modern scientific analyses clash, we become painfully aware of a third reality...*risk as politics*.[110]

Special events management requires an understanding of risk on all three of these levels. With respect to *risk as feelings,* risk perception and the fear that innocent people will fall victim to a terrorist attack is perhaps the primary reason we conduct security planning and counterterrorism preparedness activities in support of major events. Threat assessments, vulnerability assessments, and criticality assessments are the way we attempt to measure *risk as analysis* so we can construct our operational response plans accordingly. Finally, *risk as politics* comes into play when justification is required to support budget or resource requests or when risk plays a part of a powerful political agenda.

1. Risk as Feelings

The concept of risk as feelings was illustrated recently by John Tirman, executive director of the Massachusetts Institute of Technology Center for International Studies when he stated: "Is there a significant threat of a terrorist attack against America? We don't know the answer to that question, but a large number of Americans do believe there is such a threat."[111] Risk as feelings includes the perception of risk and it involves the study of affect and emotion on decision making.[112] There is a growing body of evidence that suggests that people do not make decisions based solely on empirical data such as risk probability or incident statistics. In fact, the evidence suggests that individuals make decisions in ways that differ from the rational model of choice.[113] Research confirms that individuals are predisposed to focus on negative issues and concerns because the

---

[110] Paul Slovic, Melissa l. Finucane, Ellen Peters, and Donald G. MacGregor, *Risk as Analysis and Risk as Feelings: Some Thoughts About Affect, Reason, Risk, and Rationality,* Paper presented at the annual meeting of the Society for Risk Analysis (New Orleans, LA, December 10, 2002), 3.

[111] Joe Fiorell, *Critics Slam Both U.S. Parties for Ineffective Antiterror Policies,* Global Security Newswire at http://www.nti.org/d_newswire/issues/2005_6_2.html#927C7A10 (accessed June 2, 2005).

[112] Howard Kunreuther, Robert Meyer, and Christopher Van den Bulte, *Risk Analysis for Extreme Events: Economic Incentives for Reducing Future Losses,* U.S. Department of Commerce, Open-file Report, NIST GCR 04-871, (Philadelphia, PA, October 2004), 31.

[113] Ibid., 46.

brain is wired to key in on potential and perceived threats.[114] We react with more intensity to negative experiences, and negative information is perceived as more credible than positive information.[115]

Risk as feelings is influenced by the availability heuristic, the affect heuristic, and probability neglect. The availability heuristic suggests that because negative experiences are more powerful than positive experiences, they are more easily recalled in human memory – they are more *available* to our memories. If negative images are more easily recalled, our brain makes them seem like they are more likely to occur.[116] This obviously impacts our perception of risk. The affect heuristic suggests that if something is a threat, and there is a novelty or uniqueness to it, we perceive it as a greater risk. When coupled with feelings of dread (i.e. if something appears to have a dreadful, emotional result) we see it as having greater risk, even if the likelihood of an event occurring is the same.[117] Lastly, because of the emotional and affective aspects that our sophisticated human judgment is predisposed to consider, we do not normally weigh things by the statistical likelihood they will happen. This is the essence of probability neglect.[118]

Breckenridge and Zimbardo argue that peoples' reactions are more complex than a mere visceral sense of danger to self, and multifaceted aspects of the publics' fears can strongly influence their trust in and support for government policy.[119] Kunreuther and his colleagues found that many individuals invest in security to relieve anxiety and worry about what they perceive might happen to them or to others so as to gain piece of mind.[120] Slovic, et. al. found that the *experiential system* operates in parallel with the

114 Antonio Domasio, *Descartes' error: Emotion, reason, and the human brain* (New York: Avon, 1994) in Slovic, et. al., 4.

115 James N. Breckenridge and Philip G. Zimbardo, *The Media and Disproportionate Fear,* Lecture at the Naval Postgraduate School (Monterey, CA, June 21, 2005).

116 Ibid.

117 Ibid., and Lennart Sjoberg, *The Perceived Risk of Terrorism,* SSE/EFI Working Paper Series in Business Administration No. 2002:11 (Stockholm, Sweden, January 16, 2004), 15.

118 Breckenridge and Zimbardo, *The Media and Disproportionate Fear,* Lecture June 21, 2005.

119 Ibid.

120 Kunreuther, *Risk Analysis for Extreme Events*, 47.

rational system, and that each seems to depend upon the other for guidance.[121] This suggests that much more must be considered than just the probability of an event occurring and the consequences that may result from the event.

An understanding of the nature of emotionally-based judgment and perception allows special events planners to distance themselves from the subjective influences that can impact their resource allocation decisions. It ensures that their planning efforts are not negatively influenced by a *disproportionate* fear of terrorist attack.[122] It is widely recognized that "the distinguishing feature of terrorism is fear and this fear is stimulated by threat of indiscriminant and horrifying forms of violence directed against ordinary people everywhere."[123] Recognizing the role that fear plays in terrorism allows counterterrorism professionals to focus not on *perceived* threats but rather on *actual* threats identified through comprehensive risk analysis. Recognizing that some degree of proportionate fear is warranted, however, provides a subjective check that balances the otherwise cold, objective, rational analysis.

Finally, there is a need to bring together interested parties from the private sector, representatives from public interest groups, leaders from regulatory agencies and other governmental organizations as well as representatives from the public to deal with risk management strategies.[124] This public-private integration strategy gives value beyond the scheduled special event, and it will ensure that risk management strategies are informed by a *community of experience* rather than a handful of "experts." This strategy will allow those who allocate resources for counterterrorism to more fully appreciate the difference between investing in *reassurance* versus investing in long-term strategies aimed at reducing the risk of terrorist attack or minimizing the consequences of a terrorist incident.[125]

---

[121] Slovic, et. al., *Risk as Analysis and Risk as Feelings*, 2:

[122] James N. Breckenridge and Philip G. Zimbardo, *The Strategy of Terrorism and the Psychology of Mass-mediated Fear,* Unpublished manuscript (Palo Alto, CA, 2005), 2.

[123] United Nations, *Geneva Declaration on Terrorism*, paper presented at the United Nations General Assembly (Geneva, Switzerland, May 29, 1987), in Breckenridge and Zimbardo, 4.

[124] Kunreuther, *Risk Analysis and Risk Management in an Uncertain World,* 15.

[125] Ibid., 21.

2.   Risk as Analysis

The Government Accountability Office (GAO) defines risk management as "a systematic and analytical process to consider the likelihood that a threat will endanger an asset, individual, or function and to identify actions to reduce the risk and mitigate the consequences of an attack."[126] Galway says that *risk analysis* is the process of assessing risks, while *risk management* "uses risk analysis to devise management strategies to reduce or ameliorate risk."[127]

The GAO advocates the use of a risk management approach that includes three primary elements: threat assessment, vulnerability assessment, and criticality assessment.[128] (See Figure 2). This section will address the FBI's current approach to special events management through an analysis of each of these elements, and will identify potential areas for improvement using this systematic framework.

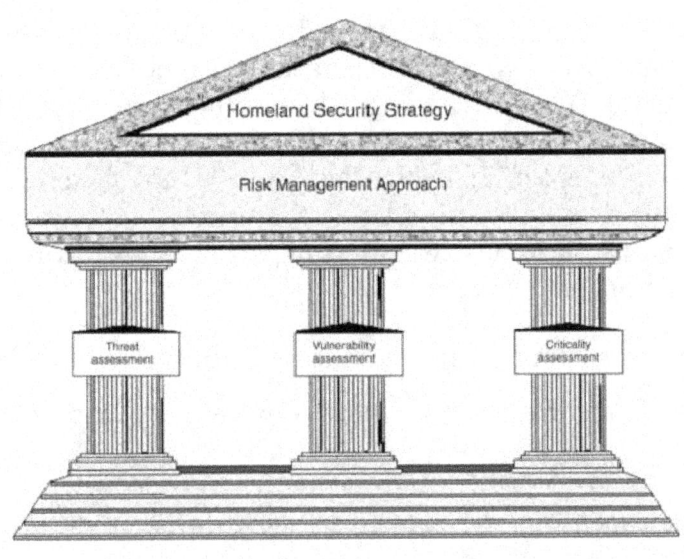

Figure 2.   GAO's three primary elements of risk management[129]

126 U.S. Government Accountability Office, *Homeland Security: Key Elements of a Risk Management Approach*, Statement of Raymond J. Decker, Director, Defense Capabilities and Management, Open-file Report, GAO-02-150T (Washington, D.C., October 12, 2001), 1.

127 Lionel Galway, *Quantitative Risk Analysis for Project Management: A Critical Review*, RAND Corporation, Open File Report, WR-112-RC, (Washington, DC., February 2004), ix.

128 Raymond Decker, *Homeland Security: Key Elements of a Risk Management Approach,* Open-file report, GAO-02-150T (Washington, D.C., October 12 , 2001), 1.

129 U.S. Government Accountability Office, *Homeland Security: A Risk Management Approach can Guide Preparedness Efforts*, Statement of Raymond J. Decker, Director, Defense Capabilities and Management, Open-file Report, GAO-02-208T, (Washington, D.C., October 31, 2001), 8.

a.   *Threat Assessment*

The FBI currently uses threat assessments to assist with some resource allocation decisions regarding special events. Individualized threat assessments are conducted for all SERL I-III events, but for all SERL IV events, planners rely upon a single, semi-annual nationwide threat assessment that is produced for all FBI offices. For NSSEs and DHS SEHS Level I events, DHS collaborates with the FBI to produce an interagency threat assessment. Because of the lack of standardization between SEHS and SERL Level I events, there may be some confusion about who is ultimately responsible for producing the threat assessments for some of the most significant special events. Differences in interagency approval processes, different timelines, and the absence of clear guidelines for what should be included in threat assessments leaves room for improvement in the current threat assessment process. The Congressional Research Service contends:

> To be helpful in assessing vulnerability and risk, threats need to be characterized in some detail. Important characteristics include type (e.g. insider, terrorist, military), or environmental (e.g., hurricane, tornado)); intent or motivation; triggers (i.e., events that might initiate an attack); capability (e.g. skills, specific knowledge, access to materials or equipment); methods (e.g., use of individual suicide bombers, truck bombs, assault, cyber): and trends (what techniques have groups used in the past or have experimented with, etc.).[130]

Ideally, threat assessments for the most significant special events should include full-spectrum, all-hazards threat information from a variety of sources known to the DHS, the FBI, and other potential sources. One of the ways to ensure a comprehensive threat assessment is to include strategic information from national intelligence and information sources as well as tactical information from the affected state and local agencies. This can be accomplished by ensuring that FBI Field Intelligence Groups (FIGs) and state fusion centers are included in the threat assessment process.

---

[130] Congressional Research Service, *Risk Management and Critical Infrastructure Protection: Assessing, Integrating, and Managing Threats, Vulnerabilities, and Consequences.* John Moteff, Specialist in Science and Technology Policy, Open-file Report RL32561 (Washington, DC, September 2, 2004), CRS-6.

FIGs are interagency intelligence working groups that are centralized within FBI field offices. They are responsible for the management, execution, and coordination of law enforcement intelligence functions. Many states have established fusion centers in an effort to centralize homeland security intelligence and information from a variety of sources including law enforcement, military, fire, weather, public health and emergency management. Building formal and informal relationships between these entities in advance of any special event is an ideal way to ensure that all actual and potential threats are adequately assessed.

The FBI currently uses a formal threat assessment process to determine whether any communicated threat is credible. This process includes evaluating the threat based on three criteria: operational practicality, technical feasibility, and behavioral resolve. When used to evaluate the threatened use of a weapon of mass destruction, for instance, the formal process includes a coordinated interagency threat assessment that evaluates not only the source of the threat but also whether the person or persons making the threat has the education, raw materials, production equipment, ability to distribute, and the motivation to carry out the threat. Extending the interagency threat assessment process to the evaluation of threats received prior to or during special events is consistent with the risk management approach. It should be formally adopted by special events planners.

By identifying and assessing threats, organizations do not have to rely on worst-case scenarios to guide planning and resource allocations. Worst case scenarios tend to focus on vulnerabilities, which are virtually unlimited, and would require extraordinary resources to address.[131] In the absence of any detailed threat information, special event planners must balance their knowledge of general threats with information about known and suspected vulnerabilities as well as information about the criticality of the targets to be protected.

b. Vulnerability Assessment

A vulnerability assessment is a process that identifies weaknesses in physical structures, personnel protection systems, processes or other areas that may be exploited by terrorists and may suggest options to eliminate or mitigate those

---

[131] Moteff, CRS-3.

weaknesses.[132] Tailored vulnerability assessments, including tactical site surveys, have long been a part of the FBI approach to special events management. The tactical site survey program was designed to manage the evaluation of physical sites for security threats and vulnerabilities, and these assessments have traditionally focused on the type of information tactical personnel require for crisis management decision making. The "all-hazards" approach to special event planning requires an approach to vulnerability assessment that goes beyond the traditional requirements of FBI special event planners. The new approach must recognize the physical, social, political, economic, cultural, and psychological harms to which individuals and modern societies are susceptible.[133] They should include a physical evaluation of the venue sites, but must also include an assessment of the anticipated participants and spectators; an understanding of supporting critical infrastructure; an assessment of the capabilities of state and local law enforcement, fire/rescue, and emergency medical services personnel; and an understanding of the assets and capabilities of all partners in the special events planning process. A worksheet recently developed by the FBI SEMU for use in collecting information during this assessment is attached at Appendix C. Vulnerability analysis should include not only addressing the items described above, it should also include exercises designed to test for further vulnerabilities. Comprehensive analysis that includes reviewing lessons learned during exercises and operations will help identify gaps that can be further assessed, prioritized, and filled.

Integration and networking are essential to the vulnerability assessment process. DHS has responsibility for the national critical infrastructure protection program, and they administer this program through the Protective Services Division (PSD) of the Infrastructure Protection Directorate. PSD has developed a robust vulnerabilities assessment tool that is useful for critical infrastructure vulnerability analysis and that may be adopted for use in special events planning. The Buffer Zone Protection Program (BZPP) was originally designed for use "outside the fence line" of

---

132 Moteff, CRS-3. 5.

133 Kunreuther, *Risk Analysis and Risk Management in an Uncertain World*, 18.

critical infrastructure targets, but it includes a comprehensive systems analysis approach that could benefit special events planners. The objectives of the BZPP are as follows:[134]

- Identify and/or enhance the existing procedures to prevent a terrorist incident at critical infrastructure/key asset facilities in the United States.

- Determine lines of communication and coordination among facilities, local, state, tribal, and federal responders.

- Conduct a gap analysis of state and local first preventers regarding equipment, staffing and training. And,

- Identify and recommend solutions to any challenges or issues regarding prevention and protective measures.

The BZPP objectives are consistent with what is required for special events planning. The BZPP includes an analysis of physical structures and other system components using the CARVER-Shock assessment methodology. This methodology provides a structured framework for documenting expert opinion about a system. The method is based on assigning a numerical value for each of a set of attributes used to describe the various complexes, components, and "nodes" of the system. Under the CARVER concept, 'system' includes the physical facilities, the commodity involved, the production processes, *and the human aspects*.[135] This type of integrated objective and subjective analysis using a structured framework is useful for understanding the complex systems in play during special events. It leverages the strengths of complementary FBI and DHS programs in a comprehensive approach to vulnerability assessment for special events – an important component of the overall risk management strategy.

c.   *Criticality Assessment*

A criticality assessment is a process designed to systematically identify and evaluate important assets and infrastructure in terms of various factors, such as the mission and significance of a target.[136] Criticality is typically defined as a measure of the consequences associated with the loss or degradation of a particular asset. The more the loss of an asset threatens the survival of those who depend on it (including the nation as a

---

134 U.S. Department of Homeland Security, *Buffer Zone Protection Program Workshop,* (Washington, D.C., November 2004).

135 Ibid.

136 GAO, *Homeland Security: A Risk Management Approach can Guide Preparedness Efforts,* 6.

whole), the more critical it becomes.[137] Criticality assessments at special events are important for a couple of reasons. At a tactical level, assessing all venue areas at a given special event is important to identify those areas of the event that are most significant or require the most resources. At a strategic level, assessing upcoming events to determine which are the most critical will assist with resource allocation decisions.

The criticality assessment is key to the sustainability of the special events management program. Without tools to determine which special events may be adequately supported by state and local officials and which events require the assistance of federal resources, the FBI and other federal agencies will be unable to effectively and efficiently deploy counterterrorism assets in support of special events.

Aside from the SERL rating system, the FBI does not currently use a criticality assessment to determine where to best allocate resources. This results in over-resourcing some events and under-resourcing others. Criticality analysis requires a risk-based needs assessment because not every event needs the same level of protection. A way to improve the criticality assessment process may be found through the reevaluation of the SERL and SEHS rating systems. An accurate SERL rating would adequately reflect the FBI's assessment of the criticality of an event. If the SERL rating were then linked to a baseline set of capabilities, such as some of those identified in the DHS Target Capabilities List, it would provide better guidance to both FBI and interagency special events planners and would clearly identify what resources could be expected from the FBI for different special events. This is discussed further in Appendix B.

The restructuring of the SERL system into a more meaningful capabilities-based assessment tool would not only improve the ability of the FBI to make resource allocation decisions, it would also go a long way toward meeting the requirements of HSPD-8 and the National Preparedness Goal.[138] The pursuit of this goal is important to the improvement of interagency preparedness and it will benefit special events as well as other potential incidents and emergencies.

---

[137] Moteff, CRS-5.

[138] President George W. Bush, *HSPD-8: National Preparedness* (December 17, 2003).

A risk analysis approach that includes the tenets of threat assessment, vulnerability assessment, and criticality assessment will improve the objectivity of the FBI special events management system and will allow FBI personnel to make more appropriate and informed resource allocation decisions in support of special events. Employment of a standardized methodology will allow FBI special event planners to articulate what criteria it uses to select events of national importance, the basic strategy it uses to determine which events warrant additional protective measures, and by how much these measures could reduce the risk to the nation.[139]

3.   Risk as Politics

Where risk as feelings and risk as analysis clash, risk as politics emerges. Members of the public and experts can disagree about risk because they define risk differently, have different worldviews, different affective experiences and reactions, or different social status.[140] Special events are inherently political. Political leaders, private and public influence-peddlers, business leaders and the media all have interests at stake in the management of special events. Additionally, the impact of interagency organizational politics cannot be discounted. An understanding of risk as politics allows special events planners to create strategies that leverage the influence of power and politics to their advantage.

In a recent article for *Global Security Newswire* it was reported that some key liberal thinkers in the U.S. believe that current U.S. antiterrorism policy keeps the populace in fear for political gain. John Tirman, the executive director of the MIT Center for International Studies was quoted as saying "...the ideology of homeland security...[creates] fear and anxiety" that boosts support for the war abroad. The Director of the Columbia University Earth Institute agreed that the U.S. populace is kept in fear and argued that if the public was better informed it would be less inclined to support military action as the primary response to the terrorist threat.[141] These comments acknowledge the role that politics plays in risk and the perception of risk, but they are focused on the negative aspects of risk as politics.

---

139 Moteff, CRS-22.

140 Paul Slovic, "Trust, Emotion, Sex, Politics, and Science: Surveying the Risk-Assessment Battlefield," *Risk Analysis* 19:4 (August 1999), 697.

141 Fiorell.

Politics can also serve a positive, functional role for special events planners. Politics can be helpful in overcoming weak leaders by ensuring that the strongest members of an organization (or coalition) are brought into positions of leadership. Politics can provide alternate channels of information and promotion and good leaders in less influential organizations can leap over poor leaders in more influential agencies or departments.[142] This can work to the benefit of an interagency plan to secure or manage a special event. An influential interagency leader who can effectively manage risk as feelings, for example, may be able to convince those with a disproportionate fear of attack to reconsider their resource allocation strategies.

Politics can also ensure that all sides of an issue are fully debated. It obliges people to fight for their preferred ideas, encouraging a variety of voices to be heard on any issue. "And because of attacks by opponents, each voice, no matter how self-serving, is forced to justify its conclusions in terms of the broader good – the interests of the organization at large."[143] Finally, politics may be required to stimulate change that is blocked by "more legitimate systems of influence…" and it can ease the path for the execution of that change. "Senior managers, for example, often use politics to gain acceptance for their decisions by building alliances to smooth their path."[144]

Understanding the political dimension of risk is important to the overall risk management strategy. Politics is only one component of the strategy, however, and the overall approach must be balanced with an understanding of risk as feelings and risk as analysis. Through the balanced application of risk management principles that includes objective and subjective inputs, political *sensitivities* may be respected and legitimately used, but political *influence* can be minimized.

---

[142] Mintzberg, Ahlstrand, and Lampel, 243.

[143] Ibid.

[144] Ibid., 244.

VII. CONCLUSIONS AND RECOMMENDATIONS

Special events are a microcosm of the world of homeland security. Effective special events management requires the elimination of duplication and overlap in favor of integration and synergy. DHS has moved quickly in its attempts to meet the goals set forth by President Bush to: "increase the capacity of the United States to prevent attacks within the United States; reduce America's vulnerability to terrorism; and minimize the damage and recover from attacks that do occur."[145] In doing so, however, DHS has created some programs and processes that have resulted in duplication of effort and contributed to confusion among local, state, and federal agencies. Ironically, this may have negatively impacted counterterrorism preparedness at major special events. The following recommendations are offered in an attempt to address this problem:

A. FOCUS ON LEADERSHIP

- **It is proposed and recommended that the FBI assume a more active leadership role in managing major special events.**

The FBI is ideally positioned to provide federal leadership in special events management by virtue of its statutory and executive authorities and mandates. The focus of special events management is currently on counterterrorism and the maintenance of public order and as such, special events are treated by state and local authorities as law enforcement problems. Legacy Presidential Decision Directives and Homeland Security Presidential Directive 5 (HSPD-5) empower the FBI to coordinate the activities of other law enforcement agencies charged with managing counterterrorism activities at special events. As the primary federal agency charged with both criminal and terrorism investigations, the FBI can leverage its unique authorities to engage in all aspects of special events coverage from planning and prevention activities to detection, deterrence and response. This is true whether or not the major special event is designated as a National Special Security Event. Additionally, the FBI has responsibilities, authorities, and resources that permit it to act globally. Regardless of whether the FBI is engaged in domestic events planning with the Department of Homeland Security or international

---

[145] President Bush, *The National Strategy for Homeland Security,* vii.

events planning with the Departments of State and Defense, the FBI is positioned to provide consistency across the federal government's special events management program.

Beyond the formal authorities that permit it to act, the FBI has the legitimacy that leaves it well prepared to assume a leadership role within the special events management community. Mintzberg, et al., describe legitimacy as a function of three systems: formal authority, established culture, and certified expertise.[146] As mentioned previously, the FBI has the appropriate authorities to act. It also has been involved in counterterrorism planning and special events management for over a decade, and a formal special events management unit has existed since 1996. The management of special events is an accepted part of the FBI's counterterrorism program. Finally, the FBI has consistently demonstrated subject matter expertise in many of the areas required for effective special events management (i.e. tactical planning, intelligence, hazardous materials response, and crisis management). In fact, the FBI special events system has served as a model to DHS and the interagency community. For these reasons, the FBI can and should assume a more proactive leadership role in counterterrorism and law enforcement planning for special events.

To demonstrate its leadership in special events, the FBI should consider the following:

- **Ensure the Special Agent in Charge (SAC) of the affected field division is personally and visibly involved in both the planning and operational aspects of major special events.**

This is essential to emphasize the importance the FBI places on counterterrorism planning and it provides confirmation to interagency partners that the FBI takes its leadership role seriously. This will also reinforce within the special events management community that the reason the FBI is involved in special events management is consistent with, and in furtherance of, the FBI's authorities and mandates. The tone set by the SAC is important to the FBI field division as well as to interagency partners. A demonstrated commitment to counterterrorism preparedness confirms that the SAC has embraced the

---

[146] Mintzberg et al., 242.

concept of terrorism prevention (proactive measures) over prosecution (reactive response). This is consistent with the new paradigm for operations in the post-September 11th world of homeland security.

The involvement of the SAC is also critical to ensure that events resourced by the FBI truly merit the allocation of planning and operational resources. The SAC serves as the "front line" in screening requests from other local, state and federal departments and agencies seeking FBI assistance. Use of the decision matrix and the planning worksheet may assist the FBI SAC in determining if the assets of the local field division can and should be used to support a proposed special event. Once the SAC determines that an event merits FBI resources, the rating system may be used to determine the level of support that is warranted.

- **Approach special events as opportunities rather than burdens.**

Often special events are seen as a burden to the law enforcement agencies charged with planning and operational response. Special events should instead be seen as opportunities and they should be embraced. Unlike exercises, in which many of the activities are either artificial or "notional," special events involve real-world scenarios with deployed personnel. They are essentially scheduled opportunities to practice real-world operational response; identify critical resource and training shortfalls; practice integration; exercise command and control; interact with the media and test media strategies; test communications systems and capture lessons learned. Special events should be used to practice the interagency interoperability skills that will be essential to any mutual aid response in a real-world crisis. As such, planning should be taken seriously and resources should be prepared in advance of special events in the same way they would be if they were to be deployed in response to a critical incident.

- **Reorganize to more effectively manage special events.**

The Special Events Management Unit (SEMU) and the Crisis Management Unit (CMU) currently conduct parallel planning for the same special events. Co-locating CMU and SEMU within the Critical Incident Response Group (CIRG) would ensure a more coordinated and comprehensive process for planning the FBI response to special events. If the units were managed from within the same operational division, specific roles and responsibilities could be more clearly defined and parallel planning processes could be more easily identified and eliminated. SEMU would have responsibility for coordinating administrative, logistical and operational planning for scheduled special events; CMU would have responsibility for coordinating contingency planning, exercises and training, interagency integration, and operational response to critical incidents that arise during scheduled special events.

- **Recast the role of FBI Headquarters special events planners to expand their oversight and operational role in special events.**

Currently, the lead responsibility for special events planning rests with field-based planners. While this focus is important, restructuring the special events program to expand the oversight and operational role of headquarters planners will improve the ability of headquarters planners to exercise their assigned program management responsibilities. Empowering headquarters personnel and increasing their visibility in operational planning will give them the insight and the legitimacy necessary to effectively address the national strategic issues that impact field operations.

Centralization of special event planning at the national level would increase consistency. It would ensure that the expertise gained in one geographic location would be transferred to other areas for future events. It would also ensure that events with the same SERL rating would be resourced similarly regardless of their location or the resources of the hosting field division. Formalizing headquarters input into local field planning efforts through appropriate process changes may also provide the national perspective necessary to balance local pressure to resource special events that may not otherwise warrant the use of FBI assets or personnel.

- **Adopt a risk management approach to special events management.**

Risks can be reduced in a number of ways: by reducing threats, by reducing vulnerabilities, or by reducing the impact or consequences.[147] By using standardized measurement criteria to determine the threats, vulnerabilities, and criticality of certain events, the FBI can make more effective choices about how it allocates its resources. Using objective tools such as the event rating level decision matrix, the planning worksheet, and rating criteria ratified by interagency partners, the FBI will be able to establish and reinforce decision-making protocols that can be used by other law

---

[147] Moteff, CRS-10.

enforcement and homeland security agencies. These protocols will allow FBI planners to articulate the criteria it uses to select events of national importance, the basic strategy it uses to determine which events warrant additional protective measures, and by how much these measures could reduce the risk to the nation.[148] This process will ensure that the FBI special events management program is rational, politically defensible, and fiscally responsible.

B. FOCUS ON THE GRAND STRATEGY

Several additional recommendations are related to the FBI's external relationships with other stakeholders. The following recommendations are aimed at improving interagency aspects of the FBI's approach to special events management. They are consistent with the three tenets of Cronin's grand strategy: *integrate*, *network*, and *balance*.

1. Integrate

Homeland Security Presidential Directive 7 (HSPD-7) states that the Secretary of Homeland Security is responsible for coordinating the overall national effort to identify, prioritize, and protect critical infrastructures and key resources, including significant special events.[149] This Directive assigned *Sector Specific Agencies* the responsibility of conducting or facilitating vulnerability assessments of their sector, and encouraging the use of risk assessment strategies to protect against or mitigate the effects of attacks against critical infrastructures or key resources.[150] The Sector Specific Agency approach works well for determining who is responsible for protecting nuclear facilities, chemical plants, power plants and other physical structures, but no Sector Specific Agency has been identified as having lead responsibility for special events management.

Clear definition of the responsibilities of DHS and the FBI with respect to special events management will allow each agency to leverage off the strengths of the other. Effective counterterrorism preparedness efforts in the post-September 11th world will require both the law enforcement authorities and experience of the FBI and the coordination mandates and abilities of DHS. This requires that the FBI be more flexible

---

[148] Moteff, CRS-22.

[149] President Bush, *HSPD-7*.

[150] Moteff, CRS-3.

and open to accepting some of the changes offered by DHS but also requires that DHS respect the legitimacy of the FBI's traditional terrorism missions, including the management of special events.

- **It is proposed and recommended that the position of Federal Coordinator (FC) be eliminated.**

The FBI Special Agent in Charge has historically been responsible for coordination of federal law enforcement and counterterrorism efforts with state and local law enforcement leaders – and the SAC will be held accountable for this responsibility. The authority and responsibility vested in the SAC is not discretionary, and it remains unchanged despite the designation of a Federal Coordinator. With the appointment of the DHS FC, (defined by DHS as the *principal* federal point of contact), it has become less clear to local, state and other federal officials with whom they should coordinate their requests for federal support for special events. It is now possible for information that previously would have been provided to the FBI SAC to be passed instead to the FC – who may or may not have control of operational assets and who may or may not be aware of the planning and operational response capabilities of the FBI field office. It is important to note that FCs are only appointed for SEHS Level I and II events, so state and local partners accustomed to dealing with the FBI SAC for the more common SEHS Level III and IV events may be especially susceptible to confusion regarding the federal special events support process.

DHS-appointed Federal Resource Coordinators (as defined in the National Response Plan) or Protective Security Advisors (PSAs) can assist the FBI SAC with overall counterterrorism planning efforts by coordinating the efforts of non-law enforcement agencies responsible for managing special events. For special events that do not involve the FBI, FRCs and PSAs can take a more active law enforcement coordination role if it is necessary. Elimination of the FC position will ensure that the efforts of response and recovery assets and law enforcement assets are coordinated, but without the duplication (and attendant confusion) that currently surrounds the FC position.

- **It is proposed and recommended that the FBI adopt the standards set forth in the National Preparedness Goal and structure its processes to be consistent with the DHS standard.**

HSPD-8 requires that all terrorism preparedness activities work toward the same overall National Preparedness Goal.[151] DHS has created the National Preparedness System to achieve that goal. It is important that the FBI immediately and fully adopt the standards set forth in the National Preparedness System to demonstrate that it has accepted DHS as a full partner in the security of the homeland, and to ensure consistency in preparedness activity throughout federal counterterrorism preparedness programs.

By incorporating the language and principles set forth in the National Response Plan (NRP) and structuring operational response elements in accordance with the National Incident Management System (NIMS), the FBI will reinforce its place as a legitimate leader in the law enforcement and homeland security community. By partnering with DHS to implement the National Infrastructure Protection Plan, improve regional collaboration, and further define the Target Capabilities List (TCL)[152] and the Universal Task List (UCL), the FBI will demonstrate its support for a common approach to national preparedness. This will show progress toward the overarching priorities identified in the DHS National Preparedness Guidance – priorities that have been identified based on their relevance to national strategic objectives and their utility in terms of high payoff contributions to national readiness.[153] The national approach to preparedness is essential in the post-September 11th world of homeland security. The graphic on the following page depicts HSPD-8 in context:

---

[151] President Bush, *HSPD-8*.

[152] U.S. Department of Homeland Security, *Target Capabilities List: Version 1.1,* Office of State and Local Government Coordination and Preparedness (Washington, D.C., May 23, 2005).

[153] U.S. Department of Homeland Security, *National Preparedness Guidance: Homeland Security Presidential Directive 8: National Preparedness* (Washington, D.C., April 27, 2005), 15.

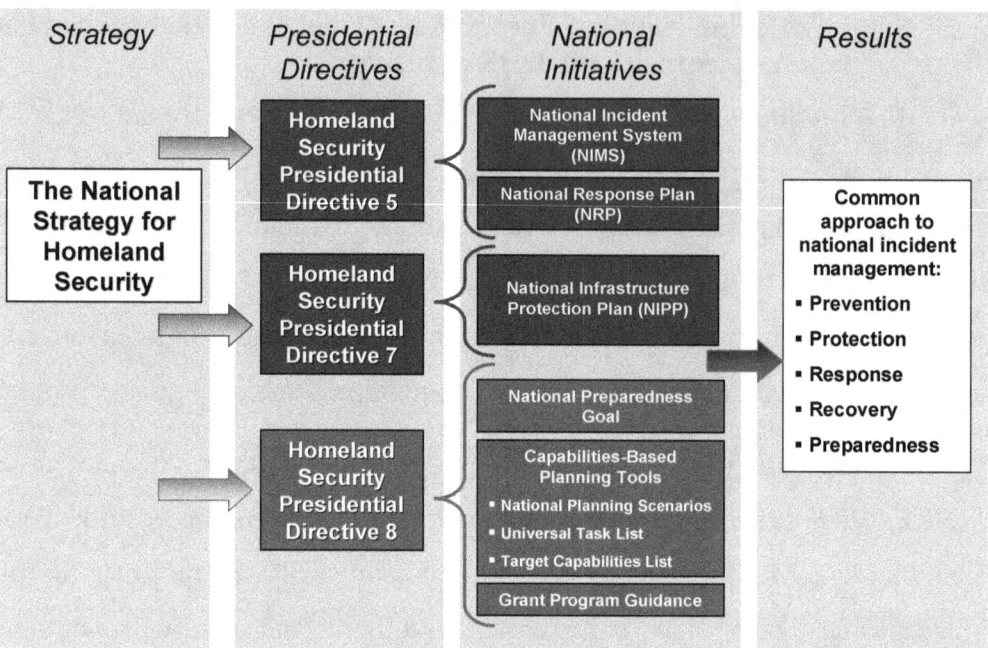

Figure 3.   HSPD-8 in Context[154]

The FBI strategy for special events management should endorse the capabilities-based planning approach that is mandated by HSPD-8 and articulated in the National Preparedness Goal. The FBI should engage in special event planning with an eye toward building the capability of each field office to manage the majority of special events. The mission of SEMU should be to tackle the major issues that are inhibiting effective field planning and to provide subject matter expertise and coordination for the major special events that are beyond the scope of the "baseline" capabilities of individual field divisions. This will ensure program consistency while at the same time allowing local planners the flexibility to adapt to local concerns.

- **It is proposed and recommended that the parallel SERL and SEHS rating systems be eliminated and that a single U.S. government special events rating system be adopted.**

Arrival at a single interagency *Special Event Assessment Rating (SEAR)* system that is developed collaboratively by the FBI and DHS and ratified by the Interagency Special Events Working Group would eliminate the confusion and duplication of effort that currently exists. Based on criteria and thresholds similar to that set forth in

[154] U.S. Department of Homeland Security, *Interim National Preparedness Goal: Homeland Security Presidential Directive 8: National Preparedness* (Washington, D.C., March 31, 2005), 2.

Appendix B, the ratings would be objective and repeatable, which makes them both rational and politically defensible. Consolidation of the parallel rating systems would have an effect on the interagency special events management community consistent with what Cronin calls "a meaningful reform of the status quo that does not necessitate wholesale organizational restructuring but that could nonetheless alleviate some of the dysfunctionalities arising from cultural conflicts and institutional rivalries."[155]

Although the SEAR levels should not be tied directly to specific federal funding, they could be tied to capabilities-based planning and the National Preparedness Goal created under HSPD-8. SEAR levels could be linked to specific priority capabilities from the TCL that have been identified as necessary for preparedness, including strengthened information sharing and collaboration; interoperable communications; improved chemical, biological, radiological, nuclear, and explosives (CBRNE) detection, response, and decontamination; and increased medical surge and mass prophylaxis capabilities.[156] In this way, local, state and federal agencies could articulate the gaps in their capabilities for managing significant special events. They could then seek additional federal grant funding or resources geared toward improving identified shortfalls. This process would allow agencies to increase their capacity to manage major special events while at the same time improve their overall preparedness posture.

- **It is proposed and recommended that FBI assets be fully integrated with other local, state, and federal assets during special events.**

A coordinated law enforcement effort is necessary to ensure a consistent and effective nationwide approach to special events management. Under the leadership of the FBI SAC, the integration of FBI assets with state and local law enforcement assets on teams responsible for all aspects of event coverage, including planning, surveillance, intelligence, identification, interview, and prosecution will provide a range of capabilities that will increase the effectiveness of all agencies involved in managing special events. The coordination of this integration under the FBI SAC is consistent with the responsibility of the FBI to coordinate the activities of other members of the law enforcement community to detect, prevent, preempt, and disrupt terrorist attacks against

---

[155] Blaise Cronin, "Intelligence, Terrorism, and National Security," *Annual Review of Information Science and Technology* 29 (2005), 415.

[156] U.S. DHS, *National Preparedness Guidance*, 15.

the United States. Once law enforcement efforts are coordinated by the FBI, DHS may coordinate the overall special event response by synthesizing the efforts of law enforcement with those of the response and recovery community. This may be accomplished by the DHS Federal Resource Coordinator (FRC), a position formally identified in the National Response Plan and recognized by members of the interagency. Specific operational integration strategies that may be useful for managing *politically charged* special events are addressed in Appendix D.

2. Network

The management of special events should be accomplished through an interagency collaborative planning approach, not a series of independent, sequential planning efforts. The U.S. Government approach currently involves separate (and independent) inputs into an overall plan to support special events. This results in a segmented product with no clear policies or standards for integration. There is little consensus on common goals and objectives. "With the rapid rise of cooperative relationships, strategy formulation leaves the exclusive confines of the single organization and becomes instead a joint process, to be developed with partners."[157] A network approach is essential to come up with a collective strategy.

- **It is proposed and recommended that the agencies consider an interagency exchange of special events planners between DHS and the FBI.**

Cronin opines "specific remedial steps that fall far short of wholesale structural reorganization might include concrete reforms aimed at reducing both intra- and interagency rivalry and segmentalism (to use Rosabeth Moss Kanter's [1983] term) such as the mixing and rotation of staff members from one agency to another – a practice not without precedence in the U.S. Intelligence community.."[158] Defense department planners have identified this as a valuable component of the overall strategy to defeat terrorist insurgency, and it may prove equally as valuable to special events management. In particular, the U.S. must be able to:

- Train personnel in a genuine interagency environment. From the classroom to daily operations to interagency training exercises, personnel must think and act as part of a network rather than a hierarchy.

---

[157] Mintzberg, Ahlstrand, and Lampel, 255.

[158] Cronin, 416.

- Develop personnel through the equivalent of military joint tours. As in the military, these tours must be an essential step for promotion…

- Operate as interagency elements down to the tactical level. This means abandoning the agency-specific stovepipes that link operations…to their U.S. headquarters.…Personnel must be trained to be effective linking into the interagency process, and those who do should be rewarded. The current process of rewarding those who do work entirely within a specific agency prevents effective networking.[159]

3. Balance

Different agencies have different core competencies and these must be fully developed for success in the post-September 11th world. Not every agency has to do everything – it is important that each understand its role in the overall counterterrorism preparedness mission. According to the FBI Strategic Plan:

> The FBI's counterterrorism successes to date have been largely determined by its flexibility, leadership, and collaboration with the U.S. Intelligence Community and its foreign and domestic law enforcement partners. Since 9/11, the FBI has: (1) shifted its counterterrorism culture and organization from reactive to proactive and "threat-based"; (2) developed a nationally-driven, fully integrated Intelligence and Investigative Program; (3) improved information sharing with other federal agencies, state and local governments, and international counterterrorism partners; (4) enhanced operational capabilities within FBI Headquarters and the field; and (5) evaluated lessons learned to better equip the nation in preventing terrorism. The FBI will continue to work closely with its intelligence and law enforcement partners focusing on full disruption of terrorist operations.

> We will also continue ongoing efforts to shift our international operations from simple liaison to dynamic operational partnerships with host country law enforcement and intelligence counterparts. Domestically, the FBI will continue to work closely with Department of Homeland Security (DHS) and community stakeholders in the counterterrorism preparedness arena — to protect the nation's critical infrastructure from attack; to protect major special events that present an operational opportunity for terrorists; to prepare against the use of WMD materiel and technology within the United States; and to focus on traditional domestic terrorism groups planning criminal acts in attempts to effect political change. [160]

---

[159] Thomas X. Hammes, "Insurgency: Modern Warfare Evolves into a Fourth Generation," *Strategic Forum* 214, (January 2005), 7.

[160] *FBI Strategic Plan 2004-2009*, 26.

The FBI, DHS, and a number of other departments and agencies all have responsibilities for counterterrorism preparedness and response. Special event planning in the post-September 11th world of homeland security does not require separate lanes of responsibility, it requires synergy of effort. Competition and dysfunction must be replaced with consensus and focus. This can only be accomplished, however, through legitimate leadership, appropriate accountability, and unity of effort. The FBI has criminal and counterterrorism mandates and authorities that make it uniquely capable of providing leadership to the law enforcement community. DHS has mandates and authorities that make it uniquely capable of coordinating the efforts of law enforcement with those of response and recovery operations. The FBI must avoid trying to expand to meet the mandates of DHS and should instead focus on its core competencies. DHS headquarters must avoid the temptation to replicate the activities of either law enforcement or response and recovery agencies and should instead focus on its coordination role. Collaboration could then become genuine as the organizations develop orientations that gradually eliminate competitive antagonism.[161]

C.   OPPORTUNITIES FOR FURTHER RESEARCH

As Homeland Security continues to emerge as an academic discipline, the area of special events management may be considered ripe for additional exploration. Little has been offered in the way of performance metrics to determine the success of special events planning. What constitutes success and how can we best determine if we have achieved it? No testing or validation of the tools offered here has yet occurred, and there is still little standardization in the way special events planners are selected and trained. Finally, technology solutions for different special events challenges are largely unexplored, including tools for situational awareness and the development of a common operating picture. While it is clear that interoperability is essential to success in special events management, the challenge lies in fully defining the players and achieving the appropriate balance among them.

D.   CONCLUSION

This thesis has identified a number of issues that require resolution if the FBI's current approach to special events management is to improve. Changes to the status quo,

---

161 Mintzberg, Ahlstrand and Lampel, 256.

mission expansion, and the increasing cost of allocating resources for special events requires that the FBI reevaluate its special events management program. This paper used several strategic planning principles to assess the FBI's current approach to special events management. It examined the subjective and objective components of the system used by the FBI and DHS to categorize and resource special events, and it concluded that the current approach is not sufficient for the post-September 11th world. The allocation of resources in support of special events requires a system that is rational, politically defensible, and fiscally responsible. A new system based on the application of risk management principles would meet these criteria.

The FBI currently engages in some aspects of risk analysis and risk management, but it has not yet formalized this process for special events management. A standardized methodology that includes an understanding of risk as feelings, risk as analysis, and risk as politics is useful for effectively managing special events. Through an integrated interagency approach that emphasizes building networks and balancing subjective and objective influences, the FBI can create a long-term, sustainable, strategic approach for its special events program that will serve as a model to the interagency special events management community.

THIS PAGE INTENTIONALLY LEFT BLANK

APPENDIX A: SWOC ANALYSIS

A strengths, weaknesses, opportunities, and challenges (SWOC) analysis of the FBI Special Events Management Unit (SEMU) was conducted to identify the external and internal issues related to SEMU's mission. This analysis was conducted as a part of an overall reevaluation of the FBI's approach to Special Events management in the post-9/11 world. Consistent with the framework identified by Bryson, four questions were addressed during the SWOC analysis.[162]   The questions and the results of the SWOC analysis are listed below:

What major external or future opportunities are available to the FBI?

- Changes in DHS leadership may leave the FBI better positioned to influence the direction of the interagency Special Events management community. Michael Chertoff, Secretary of the Department of Homeland Security, recently declared, "This is a marathon, not a sprint...we must lay out a vision of homeland security is sustainable over the long run."[163] He has mandated a review of DHS programs and initiatives to identify and eliminate areas of overlap, ineffectiveness and inefficiency.
- There is a lull in scheduled major events this year, allowing time for the completion of major projects (i.e. completion of the update to the Special Events management handbook; increased communication and liaison with FBI field offices; better collaboration with interagency partners).
- There has been more focus on special events management, especially as it relates to counterterrorism, since 9/11 (there is a need for a *community* of experts)
- The FBI has long had a rating system in place that provides a guideline for how to respond to and resource special events (Special Event Readiness Level (SERL) system). This historical reference is valuable to the interagency community (especially DHS) as it develops a similar system for allocating resources in support of special events.
- HSPD-8 requires that agencies engage in capabilities-based planning.[164]   This requirement affords SEMU an

---

[162] Ibid., 141.

[163] Michael Chertoff, *Remarks for Secretary Michael Chertoff, U.S. Department of Homeland Security, George Washington University Homeland Security Policy Institute,* (Washington, D.C., March 16, 2005) at http://www.dhs.gov/dhspublic/display?theme=44&content=4391 (accessed June 11, 2005).

[164] President Bush, *HSPD-8.*

opportunity to review its current strategies for FBI Special Events management to determine where/how SEMU can increase its effectiveness.

What major external or future challenges are facing the FBI?

- There has been no clear delineation of responsibilities (or authorities) of the agencies involved in planning and operational response during special events. Consequently, FBI authorities may be perceived as being in conflict with the authorities and responsibilities of other agencies.
- Agency policies are sometimes interpreted to have the same force of law as legislative authorities/mandates – this further confuses the lanes of responsibility.
- If homeland security grants are coupled to SERL or Special Events Homeland Security (SEHS) rating systems, political pressure to rate events at levels higher than they warrant may artificially inflate the ratings. This is fiscally dangerous.
- As budget formulas are revised and reevaluated, agencies are increasingly being forced to compete for scarce resources. Some agencies are expanding into homeland security and counterterrorism in an attempt to leverage more resources – even though they may have not historically held those missions. At least some of that expansion has been into areas of special event management that have traditionally been part of the mission of the FBI. (Turf wars and rice bowls).
- Current threats require a cultural shift on the part of the FBI. Information sharing and inclusion must replace information collection and exclusion if current counterterrorism strategies are going to succeed.

What are the FBI's major internal or present strengths?

- Many employees in SEMU have garnered a great deal of experience and expertise in special events management, especially within the past year.
- New employees have demonstrated an interest in learning about special events management (they appear poised to take ownership in new programs).
- Most of the new employees have strong operational backgrounds.
- New leadership in the SEMU has significant background in liaison and interagency issues, and significant operational experience.

72

- The FBI has a large repository of information about lessons learned at special events – a huge library from which to draw upon to improve the way special events are managed.

What are the FBI's major internal or present weaknesses?

- The Special Events program is managed within the Weapons of Mass Destruction/Domestic Terrorism Operations Section, and it is considered less important than some other programs in the Section.
- The unit has acquired a reputation as a means of financial support, but not necessarily operational support.
- There is lack of clarity on how SEMU contributes to the counterterrorism community.
- There have been few attempts to exploit the information that exists in historical files to get a comprehensive picture of the past so that it can inform the future.
- Despite significant institutional experience managing special events, no template has emerged that provides guidance to new special events planners about how to do "typical" events (i.e. large sporting events vs. politically charged special events).
- FBI Special Events planning is decentralized and most events are planned by different field divisions "from the ground up" each time. This may result in some resources being allocated based on political or subjective decisions. There exists a need for an objective analysis of which events should be supported, and to what degree they should be resourced.

THIS PAGE INTENTIONALLY LEFT BLANK

APPENDIX B: EVENT RATING LEVEL DECISION MATRIX

It is recognized that formal interagency reconciliation of the SERL and SEHS rating systems is necessary if a single U.S. government system for rating and resourcing special events is to be developed. The following decision matrix is offered as a starting point for that discussion. The matrix lists the definitions used by both the FBI and DHS for determining their special event rating levels. Threshold numbers were initially developed for SERL criteria only, and they were derived primarily based upon the author's experience. The values were then vetted by a small focus group comprised of FBI special events management experts and tested for validity against historical FBI SERL I, II, III, and IV special events cases.

After the criteria were determined to be valid for the SERL rating system, additional criteria values were developed for the three additional SEHS criteria. These values are offered as placeholders only. No vetting or testing has been conducted on the criteria values for SEHS criteria because they may not be consistent with other rating systems that are currently being developed by DHS to evaluate critical infrastructure and/or domestic preparedness.

The numbers assigned to each of the threshold levels in the matrix (in parentheses) do not correspond directly to SERL or SEHS rating levels. They are simply values used to determine an overall numeric score. The final SERL or SEHS rating is derived by dividing the overall score (sum of the criteria values) by the number of rating criteria values used (8 for SERL system and 11 for SEHS system). The raw score is then converted to the corresponding SERL or SEHS level. The results are as follows:

Total score / 8 = Raw Score

Raw Score	SERL Level
0.0-2.5	SERL IV
2.5-3.0	SERL III
3.0-3.5	SERL II
3.5+	SERL I

Total score/11 = Raw Score

Raw Score	SEHS Level
0.0-2.5	SEHS IV
2.5-3.0	SEHS III
3.0-3.5	SEHS II
3.5+	SEHS I

SERL Rating System Criteria	SEHS Rating System Criteria
Size: This includes the size of both the event and the responsible field office. The greater the number of participants and associated staff, generally the greater the security and safety requirement. Size of the field office is also an important consideration as larger offices may be able to absorb the resource requirements for supporting an event more readily than smaller offices. **Size – Participants and Sponsors** **0-100 (1)** **100-500 (2)** **500-1000 (3)** **1000+ (4)** **Size – FBI Field Office** **Large – 12 (1)** **Medium – 34 (2)** **Small – 10 (3)** **Legal Attache (LEGAT) (4)**	Size: Factors include the size of the event, including multiplicity of jurisdictions involved and the number of participants and associated staff. Larger events are more likely to draw attention of terrorists, or other criminals, seeking to cause mass casualties.
Threat: Relevant considerations include the state of global political affairs, current domestic and global terrorist activity levels, previous acts of terrorism or other violence associated with this event, threats associated with similar events, current threat directed toward this event or attendees, and the realistic degree of danger that known terrorist groups may pose to the event. **Threat Level** **No articulable threat (1)** **Homeland Security Code Yellow (2)** **General, but articulable threat (3)** **Specific threat (4)**	Threat: Factors include current threats directed toward this event or attendees; current threats associated with similar events; current levels of domestic and global terrorist activity; previous terrorist incidents or acts of violence associated with the event or similar events; the threat assessment for terrorism and civil disturbance before, during, and after the event; and the state of global political affairs – geopolitical considerations.
Significance: Some events have historical, political, and/or symbolic significance that heightens concern about associated terrorist or other criminal activity. **Significance** **Local (1)** **Regional (2)** **National (3)** **International (4)**	Significance: The symbolic, political and/or historical significance of the event.
Duration: Longer events often require more resources than those of relatively short duration. **Duration** **1 day (1)** **2-3 days (2)** **Up to 7 days (3)** **7+ days (4)**	Duration: The duration of the event. Events lasting for an extended period of time often require more resources than those of relatively short duration and they potentially provide more opportunities for attack.

Location: An event's location may provide an attractive stage for a criminal or terrorist act. Certain locations may require unique capabilities to ensure adequate event security. The geographical dispersion of an event is also an important consideration when determining resource requirements. **Location** **Rural (1)** **Suburban (2)** **Urban (3)** **Urban Area Security Initiative (4)**	Location: The location of the event may provide an attractive stage for a criminal or terrorist act. This factor includes assessment of the capability of Federal, state, and local resources available to support the event. If it is a recurring event, local agencies are more experienced. Certain locations may require unique capabilities to ensure adequate event security. The geographical dispersion of an event is also an important consideration when determining resource requirements
Attendance: Major events may have a large number of spectators in a relatively confined space, providing an inviting target for various weapons of mass destruction (WMD). Attendees may also include people from disparate cultural, political, and religious backgrounds, some of whom may have antagonistic relationships. **Attendance** **0-25,000 (1)** **25,000-50,000 (2)** **50,000-100,000 (3)** **100,000+ (4)**	Attendance: The number and type of attendees/participants. Major events may have a large number of spectators in a relatively confined space, providing an inviting target for terrorist attacks (i.e. WMD). Attendees may include people from disparate cultural, political, and religious backgrounds, some of whom may have antagonistic relationships.
Media Coverage: Live media coverage presents terrorists and other criminal elements with a lucrative forum for making a statement to a wide audience. Events with national and/or international media attention, therefore, may provide a more attractive target than those with minimal coverage. **Media Coverage** **Local (1)** **Regional (2)** **National (3)** **International (4)**	Media coverage: Focus of national and/or international media attention on the event. Live media coverage presents terrorists and other criminal elements with a lucrative forum for making a statement to a wide audience. Events with national and/or international media attention may provide a more attractive target than those with minimal coverage.
Dignitaries: Large events may draw numerous government officials and other dignitaries from around the nation and the world. Domestic and international criminal elements may be attracted to these individuals because of who they are, what they represent, or merely because they are well. **Dignitaries in Attendance** **None known (1)** **Mayor/Governor/Regional Celebrity (2)** **Foreign Minister/National Celebrity/Former Head of State (3)** **Current Head of State (4)**	Dignitaries: Participation by high-level U.S. and/or foreign government officials. Large events may draw numerous government officials and other dignitaries from around the nation and the world. Domestic and international criminal elements may be attracted to government officials and dignitaries. The number and rank of the attending officials may affect the assessment of the potential threat and the level of the security deemed necessary.

77

Not currently defined by the FBI.	Federal sponsorship or participation: Events with Federal presence may present an attractive target for terrorist acts. Such events are also likely to be high profile and of national significance, therefore also attractive to terrorists. This includes consideration of both the level and complexity of Federal capabilities employed. **Federal Sponsorship or Participation** **Federal participation – nominal (1)** **Federal participation – significant (2)** **Federal sponsorship – low profile (3)** **Federal sponsorship – high profile (4)**
Not currently defined by the FBI.	Critical infrastructure: Proximity of critical infrastructure. The number, density, and vulnerability of critical infrastructure sites in proximity to the venue must be considered. **Critical Infrastructure in Proximity** **Low vulnerability/low consequence (1)** **High vulnerability/low consequence (2)** **Low vulnerability/high consequence (3)** **High vuln. /high consequence (4)**
Not currently defined by the FBI.	State and local capabilities: Size and expertise of state and local police forces, other responders. Adequacy of security capabilities at the state and local level. Adequacy of other state and local resources. Request by state or local agencies for Federal assistance. **State and Local Capabilities** **Large - >500 sworn personnel (1)** **Medium - 100-500 sworn personnel (2)** **Small - <100 sworn officers/personnel (3)** **No Capability - (4)**

Table 3.   Special Event Rating Level Decision Matrix

It is proposed and recommended that the parallel SERL and SEHS rating systems be eliminated and that a single U.S. government special events rating system be adopted. Arrival at a single interagency *Special Event Assessment Rating (SEAR)* system that is developed collaboratively by the FBI and DHS and ratified by the Interagency Special Events Working Group would eliminate the confusion and duplication of effort that currently exists. Based on criteria and thresholds similar to those set forth above, the ratings would be objective and repeatable, which makes them both rational and politically defensible.

This matrix presumes that an event planner has determined that the event potentially qualifies for federal assistance. Historically the Special Agent in Charge of an

FBI field office determines if an event qualifies for FBI assistance, and he or she has the authority to designate an event as a SERL IV. It is assumed that each federal agency using this decision matrix will conduct a basic inquiry to confirm that the agency has the authority and jurisdiction to provide the contemplated support.

There is a subjective component to special event planning that does not lend itself to quantifiable analysis. For that reason, this matrix is offered only as a guideline. If aggravating or mitigating factors exist that cannot be measured adequately by the criteria in the matrix, the event should be evaluated by potential stakeholders via an appropriate interagency assessment forum such as the Special Events Working Group.

Although the SEAR levels should not be tied directly to specific federal funding, they could be tied to capabilities-based planning and the National Preparedness Goal created under HSPD-8. SEAR levels could be linked to specific capabilities from the DHS Target Capabilities List (TCL) identified as necessary for special event preparedness. In this way, local, state and federal agencies could articulate the gaps in their capabilities for managing significant special events. Agencies could then seek additional federal grant funding or resources geared toward improving identified shortfalls.

THIS PAGE INTENTIONALLY LEFT BLANK

APPENDIX C: FBI PRE-EVENT PLANNING WORKSHEET

I.   **BACKGROUND INFORMATION**

Name of event: _____

Date(s) of event: _____

Number of venues: _____

(Note: **In this document, "venue" refers to a specific facility or location, and "site" refers to a city or State)**

Location of event (Primary Venue): _____
City: _____   State: _____

Name of State Homeland Security Director (or designee): _____

POINT OF CONTACT (LAW ENFORCEMENT OFFICIAL) FOR SECURITY ISSUES:

Name: _____

Title: _____

Agency: _____

Address: _____

City: _____   State: _____

Email Address: _____

Phone Number: _____   Fax: _____

Cellular Number: _____

II.   LOGISTICAL INFORMATION

1.   Name of event host organization: _____

2.   Type of organization hosting event:

☐ Government   ☐ Private (non-government)

☐ State/Local   ☐ National   ☐ International

3.   Type of event: ☐ Sporting   ☐ Political   ☐ Educational   ☐ Business

☐ Cultural   ☐ Other

If other, please describe: _____

4.   Number of spectators anticipated: _____

Estimated number of participants: _____

Foreign countries expected to participate: _____

Estimated number of foreign participants: _____

Press/Media (both print and broadcast): _____

_____

_____

Dignitaries/VIPs (U.S. and foreign) accompanied by protective security details:

Name of Dignitary/VIP	Title or Function at Event	Type of Security		
		☐ Federal	☐ State/local	☐ Private
		☐ Federal	☐ State/local	☐ Private
		☐ Federal	☐ State/local	☐ Private
		☐ Federal	☐ State/local	☐ Private

5.   If the event has been held previously, provide the dates and locations: _____

_____

_____

_____

_____

6.   Are there secondary venues?   ☐ yes   ☐ no   If yes, please list:

(Note: In this document, "venue" refers to a specific facility or location, and "site" refers to a city or State)

82

Name of Venue	Address

7. Is the event occurring at multiple sites? ☐ yes ☐ no   If yes, please list:

Name of Site	Address

8. Will the events at multiple sites run concurrently? ☐ yes ☐ no   If yes, please list:

9. Are there any other events or circumstances occurring at the same time as this event that could draw upon similar State and local law enforcement and public safety resources?

☐ yes ☐ no
If yes, please describe: _____
_____
_____

10. Additional event and site information (if necessary): _____
_____
_____
_____

III.   OPERATIONAL INFORMATION

1.   List all federal, state or local public safety agencies involved in planning (include State National Guard, if appropriate):

Lead	Name of Agency and Contact Person	Type of Agency	Estimated number of personnel involved in event
☐			
☐			
☐			

☐			

2.   Will non-sworn personnel be involved in security for this event? ☐ yes ☐ no If yes how many will be:

    a. Private Security personnel: _____   b. Volunteer Security personnel: _____

    c. National Guard personnel: _____   d. Other: _____

    If other, please describe: _____

3.   Has a request been submitted to conduct name checks for this event? ☐ yes ☐ no; if so,

    a. Approximately how many names will be submitted for checks? _____

    b. What types of checks have been requested? (i.e., CIA, ICE, NCIC, ACS, etc.) _____
    _____
    _____
    _____

4.   What criteria have been established regarding credentialing for the event? _____
    _____
    _____
    _____

5. List any committees that have been formed and the agencies and organizations represented on each, including the FBI:

Name of Committee	Agencies Represented

Name of Committee	Agencies Represented

6.   Have subcommittees been established to coordinate the following (X all that apply):

☐	Accreditation	☐	HazMat/WMD
☐	After Action	☐	Host Liaison
☐	Airspace Security	☐	Intelligence
☐	Budget & Logistics	☐	Interagency Communication
☐	Civil Disobedience	☐	Legal
☐	Contingency Planning	☐	Media Relations
☐	Consequence Management	☐	Physical Security
☐	Crisis Management	☐	Tactical Assets
☐	Cyber & Critical Infrastructure Security	☐	Transportation
☐	Executive Protection	☐	Workforce Preparedness/Training
☐	Hazardous Devices	☐	Crisis Negotiations

7.   What additional subcommittees have been established?

Name of Subcommittee	Name of Subcommittee

8.   Have subcommittee mission statements, goals and timetables been established? ☐ yes ☐ no

9.   Are FBI representatives from the Field Office participating in subcommittees? ☐ yes ☐ no
        If yes, provide the following:

Name of Subcommittee	FBI Representative

Name of Subcommittee	FBI Representative

10.   Will a Joint Operations Center (or similar interagency command post) be activated for this event?

       ☐ yes   ☐ no

If yes, provide the location: _____

11.   Will a Joint Information Center (or similar public/media liaison center) be activated for this event?

       ☐ yes   ☐ no

If yes, provide the location: _____

12.   Will an Intelligence Operations Center (or similar interagency intelligence center) be activated for this event?

       ☐ yes   ☐ no

If yes, provide the location: _____

13.   Will a Bomb Management Center (or similar interagency center) be activated for this event?

       ☐ yes   ☐ no

If yes, provide the location: _____

14.   Have any of the following training exercises directly related to this event already occurred or been scheduled to occur (X all that apply):

☐   Tabletop exercise

If yes, provide date, location and participants: _____

_____

_____

_____

☐   Joint Field Training Exercise

If yes, provide date, location and participants: _____

_____

_____

_____

☐   Other training (i.e., CPX, Crisis Management, NIMS/NRP, ICON)

If yes, provide date, location and participants: _____

_____

_____

_____

15. Do State and Local LE agencies have the resources and training necessary to respond to possible incidents of mass protest and civil disobedience? ☐ yes ☐ no

16. Discuss any other pertinent security information: _____
_____
_____
_____

III. TACTICAL INFORMATION AND COORDINATION

<u>Point of Contact</u> (law enforcement official) for security issues:

Name: _____

Title: _____

Agency: _____

Address: _____

City: _____   State: _____

Email Address: _____

Phone Number: _____   Fax: _____

Cellular Number: _____

1. Has an incident command system been adopted for this site?   ☐ yes ☐ no

2. Will the local emergency operations center, separate from the joint operations center, be activated?

    ☐ yes   ☐ no   If yes, provide the following information:

    a. Describe the coordination relationship between the EOC and the JOC:_____
    _____
    _____
    _____

    b. List Agencies or Emergency Support Functions (ESFs) that will be activated or on standby for this event:

Agency or ESF	Agency or ESF

3. List the approximate number of tactical personnel, i.e. SWAT, available from the jurisdictions (Local/State) that could be called upon to support the event:

Agency/Team	Number of Tactical Personnel

4. List the approximate number of Crisis Negotiations personnel available from the jurisdictions (Local/State) that could be called upon to support the event?

Agency/Team	Number of Tactical Personnel

5. Does the event jurisdiction have a hazardous materials response capability? ☐ yes ☐ no

   a. List the agent detection and identification capabilities of the Team(s) (include response for chemical, biological and radiological/nuclear):

Detection and Identification Capabilities	Detection and Identification Capabilities

   b. List the mass decontamination capabilities of the Team(s):

Mass Decontamination Capabilities	Mass Decontamination Capabilities

   c. Are hospital facilities dependent upon local hazardous materials teams for their facility's patient/mass decontamination capabilities? ☐ yes ☐ no

d. List all local hospitals and their proximity to the event:

Hospital	Proximity to the Event

6. Does the event jurisdiction have an Improvised Explosive Device Disposal response capability?

☐ yes ☐ no

a. Is the Render Safe Team accredited? ☐ yes ☐ no
If yes, how many certified technicians does the Render Safe Team have? _____

b. How many fully equipped Response Teams (minimum of 2 Bomb Techs) can the event jurisdiction   dispatch at the same times? _____

c. Can the Render Safe Team respond to a WMD incident in appropriate protective equipment

(SRS-5 with SCBA)? ☐ yes ☐ no
If yes, how many personnel are trained at this level? _____

d.   Does the Render Safe Team(s) have portable containment vessels?   ☐ yes   ☐ no
If yes, how many? _____

e. Does the Render Safe Team(s) have portable X-ray machines? ☐ yes   ☐ no
If yes, how many? _____

f. Does the Render Safe Team(s) have a robotics capability? ☐ yes   ☐ no
If yes, how many? _____

7. List the number of certified bomb technicians (State/Local) who could be called upon to support the event:

Agency/Team	Number of certified bomb technicians

8. List local teams or capabilities (HazMat, EMS, US&R) that will be activated or on standby for this event:

Local Team/Capability	Local Team/Capability

9.   List local Urban Search and Rescue capabilities that will be activated or on standby for this event:

Local Team/Capability	Local Team/Capability

10.   List Public Health assets/capabilities that will be deployed or on standby for this event:

Local Team/Capability	Local Team/Capability

11.   List the local laboratory and testing facilities and their capabilities: _____
_____
_____
_____
_____

12.   Will the State emergency operations center be activated? ☐ yes   ☐ no

    a.   Dates of activation: _____

    b.   Hours of operation: _____

    c.   EOC Director/Point of Contact: _____

13.   List the agencies or Emergency Support Functions that will be activated at the EOC for the event:

Agency or ESF	Agency or ESF

14.   List State Agencies, Teams or capabilities that will be activated or on standby for the event:

State Team/Capability	State Team/Capability

15.   Will a Temporary Flight Restriction (TFR) be requested for this event? ☐ yes   ☐ no

16.   If the event was held previously, was a TFR approved? ☐ yes   ☐ no

17. Are there any anticipated issues surrounding the TFR request for this event? ☐ yes ☐ no
If yes, please describe in detail: _____
_____
_____

18. List any anticipated State and local tactical capability shortfalls for which you may request Federal support:

State and Local Capability Shortfall	State and Local Capability Shortfall

III. TECHNICAL INFORMATION

1. Are communications systems interoperable among various consequence management, critical incident management and law enforcement components? ☐ yes ☐ no

Describe: _____
_____
_____
_____

2. Are communications systems interoperable among public health, hospital and medical facilities? ☐ yes ☐ no
Describe: _____
_____
_____
_____

3. FBI Radio System

a. Has a radio communications frequency plan been developed? ☐ yes ☐ no

b. Will temporary radio repeaters be required at the primary venue? ☐ yes ☐ no

c. Will temporary radio repeaters be required at any secondary venues? ☐ yes ☐ no

4. FBI Computer System
a. Will additional computer capabilities be required at the following locations; If yes, please describe:

1) JOC? _____
_____
_____
_____

2) JIC? _____
_____
_____
_____

3)   IOC? _____

_____

_____

_____

b. Will FBINET computers be utilized at the primary venue? ☐ yes ☐ no
   At the following locations:

    1) JOC?☐ yes ☐ no

    2) JIC? ☐ yes ☐ no

    3) IOC?☐ yes ☐ no

c. Will the ICON system be utilized for this event? ☐ yes ☐ no
If so, how many ICON facilitators will be required? _____

d. Will the LEO Virtual Command Post be utilized? ? ☐ yes ☐ no

3.   <u>Electrical Power</u>

a. Will additional power outlets be required at the following locations; If yes, please describe:

    1) JOC? _____

_____

_____

_____

    2) JIC? _____

_____

_____

_____

    3) IOC? _____

_____

_____

_____

b. Describe in detail any existing emergency electrical power system at the following locations:

    1) JOC? _____

_____

_____

_____

    2) JIC? _____

_____

_____

_____

    3) IOC? _____

_____

_____

_____

c. Will an electrical transfer switch between grid and generator power be required? If yes, at what locations? _____

_____
_____
_____

4.   Telephone System

    a. Will additional telephone lines be required at any of the following locations:

        1)   JOC?   ☐ yes ☐ no

        2)   JIC?   ☐ yes ☐ no

        3)   IOC?   ☐ yes ☐ no

    b. Will high speed Internet service be required at any of the following locations:

        1)   JOC?   ☐ yes ☐ no

        2)   JIC?   ☐ yes ☐ no

        3)   IOC?   ☐ yes ☐ no

5.   Video

    a. Will video feeds from existing or planned city cameras from local agencies be directed to the following:

        1)   JOC?   ☐ yes ☐ no

        2)   JIC?   ☐ yes ☐ no

        3)   IOC?   ☐ yes ☐ no

IV.   INTELLIGENCE INFORMATION

1.   Has an interagency intelligence information sharing system been established for this event?

    ☐ yes   ☐ no

2.   Will a joint intelligence center (or similar interagency intelligence center) be activated for this event?

    ☐ yes   ☐ no

3.   Describe any known threats or concerns regarding public safety, as related to this event: _____

_____
_____
_____
_____

4.   Describe any historical, political, economic or other significant factors that may attract criminal activity or terrorism to this event: _____

_____
_____
_____
_____

5. Are demonstration permit requests anticipated for this event? ☐ yes ☐ no
   If yes, provide details: _____
   _____
   _____
   _____
   _____

6. Have demonstration permits been requested for this event? ☐ yes ☐ no
   If yes, list below:

Name of Group Requesting Demonstration Permit	Type of Activity (e.g., rally, parade)	Number of Participants	Permit Approved
			☐ Yes ☐ No
			☐ Yes ☐ No
			☐ Yes ☐ No
			☐ Yes ☐ No
			☐ Yes ☐ No

7. What has been (or is anticipated to be) the scope of the media attention for this event (both print and broadcast)?

   ☐ none ☐ minimal (State & Local only) ☐ significant (national) ☐ international

8. Additional intelligence information: _____
   _____
   _____
   _____
   _____

THIS PAGE INTENTIONALLY LEFT BLANK

APPENDIX D: INTEGRATION OPTIONS FOR MANAGING POLITICALLY CHARGED SPECIAL EVENTS

The following discussion is offered to demonstrate some of the possible options for integrating FBI resources with other local, state, and federal authorities charged with managing special events.   The integration strategies are addressed in the context of politically charged special events (PCSEs) because there are specific concerns with respect to PCSEs that make these events particularly challenging for the FBI. Many of the strategies outlined for managing PCSEs may be applied to major sporting events, National Special Security Events, and other significant special events.

PCSEs require a law enforcement response that is different than other special events because PCSEs have wide-reaching political or social impact and they often occur within a highly-polarized environment. Because of their nature, PCSEs tend to receive extensive media attention; they often draw large numbers of protestors and demonstrators; and they require a significant number of local, state, and federal law enforcement resources.

Changing tactics within the anti-globalization movement,[165] the shifting focus of law enforcement priorities from prosecution to prevention, and a preoccupation with terrorism throughout all levels of government has renewed the debate over how aggressively law enforcement should pursue internal dissent and the domestic groups and individuals that use violence in furtherance of their political or social goals. Injuries to law enforcement officers during protest events and significant property damage at several large-scale demonstrations have prompted police to spend more time and more resources planning for PCSEs. The recognition that there exists a small number of individuals who travel in interstate commerce with the express purpose of committing violent acts during public demonstrations suggests that a more strategic approach to managing these events

---

[165] Robert Weissman, "Puppets, Protestors and Police: April 16 Mobilization Builds Momentum against the IMF and World Bank," *Multinational Monitor* 21, no. 5 (May 2000), 24-29 at http://www.proquest.com/ (Accessed May 24, 2004).

may be necessary. Unfortunately, national planning efforts have not been effectively coordinated and no nationwide strategy has emerged for targeting this mobile criminal problem.

Local law enforcement officials are primarily responsible for policing PCSEs, but the FBI can play a significant role in assisting with these events. The FBI has a nationwide presence that can provide consistency for a national strategy aimed at disrupting the criminal groups that travel between states to commit criminal activity at PCSEs. For this strategy to succeed, however, the FBI must effectively integrate with its law enforcement partners.

A.   INTEGRATED PLANNING TEAMS

The establishment of integrated planning teams that represent law enforcement at the local, state and federal level increases the efficiency of the planning process and the effectiveness of the operational response to PCSEs. The integration of FBI agents in all aspects of planning, including the initial meetings with demonstration organizers, will show there is a clear, deliberate, consistent strategy that will be implemented by law enforcement authorities. Local officials, in conjunction with state and federal officials, should clearly articulate conditions for demonstrations and should provide accepted standards of conduct in advance of any PCSE. Acceptable standards of conduct would include any form of legal, non-violent activity. It should be made clear that illegal, non-violent conduct will be managed by the local authorities, but that any illegal, violent conduct *may also* result in a response by federal law enforcement authorities.

B.   INTEGRATED OPERATIONAL TEAMS

Joint Terrorism Task Forces (JTTFs) have demonstrated that integration of local, state, and federal investigative resources results in collective tools that far exceed the capabilities of any one of the components. The task force approach has been extremely successful because it enables investigators to approach criminal and terrorism cases from a number of different perspectives. Using investigative task forces to conduct appropriately predicated investigations on those who travel between states expressly to commit violence during public demonstrations is an essential component of a national strategy aimed at managing PCSEs.

Field Intelligence Groups (FIGs) are interagency intelligence working groups that are centralized within FBI field offices. They are responsible for the management, execution, and coordination of law enforcement intelligence functions. Integrating the FIGs with state and local law enforcement authorities responsible for policing PCSEs is an ideal way to coordinate intelligence activities. The FBI has a large amount of strategic intelligence concerning groups and individuals involved in illegal behavior, including those who engage in violent activity at protest events. State and local authorities are usually better positioned to provide tactical intelligence that confirms the presence of known violent actors and their activities in local areas. The coordination of intelligence collection and distribution efforts through a single *Intelligence Operations Center (IOC)* results in a common operating picture that provides better intelligence coverage for the current event. This approach also fosters legacy intelligence that can be used for future events.

Other successful operational integration concepts that have been used at recent PCSEs are the *Joint Hazardous Assessment Teams* (JHATs) and *Joint Hazardous Explosive Response Teams* (JHERTs). The *JHATs* are interagency teams consisting of local, state, and federal hazardous materials specialists who respond to and assess potential hazardous materials incidents. The *JHERTs* are interagency teams consisting of local, state, and federal explosive ordnance technicians who respond to and assess suspicious packages and improvised explosive devices. Joint interagency teams generally have a larger number of tools at their disposal and they often have inter-jurisdictional authority contained within a single response element. JHATs and JHERTs are uniquely prepared to respond to the most common technical incidents that arise at PCSEs.

C.   INTEGRATED DOCUMENTATION AND PROSECUTION TEAMS

Local and federal law enforcement officials gather evidence and prepare cases according to different rules. The adoption of integrated evidence collection, arrest, identification and interview procedures will result in better documentation of individual criminal activity at PCSEs. Thorough identification of individual arrestees and clear documentation of their specific criminal acts increases the likelihood that individuals who resort to violence will be held accountable for their actions. This may translate to more criminal convictions, more accurate criminal history records, and more effective collection of criminal intelligence for all levels of law enforcement.

Cases that arise out of PCSEs that have potential for federal prosecution should be developed cooperatively for presentation to both state and federal prosecutors. Task forces consisting of law enforcement officers and prosecutors from state and federal agencies should collectively determine whether violent criminal acts that occur at PCSEs would be most effectively addressed by state or federal courts. Development of a clear strategy for prosecution is essential to the coordinated national effort aimed at reducing the recurring violence associated with PCSEs.

One of the benefits of aggressively prosecuting crimes that occur at PCSEs is that certain crimes qualify as *predicate offenses* for more complex racketeering prosecutions. Appropriately documenting predicate offenses increases the options available for use against the violent criminal actors who travel between states to commit violent criminal activity at multiple PCSEs. Subsequent crimes can be investigated as part of a terrorism enterprise investigation,[166] and they may be prosecuted under the antiracketeering statutes, which include the Racketeer Influenced and Corrupt Organizations (RICO) Act.[167] RICO prosecutions may prove especially useful for dismantling the organizations that continually seek to disrupt PCSEs through violent action.

D. INTEGRATED COMMAND AND CONTROL

1. Unified Command

State and local authorities have responsibility for security, crowd control and public safety during mass demonstrations. Day-to-day special event management activities are coordinated by state and local authorities consistent with the precepts of the National Incident Management System (NIMS).[168] Local and state law enforcement commanders generally use a concept known as *Unified Command* to ensure interagency situational awareness and to coordinate the overall law enforcement response. FBI command and control assets can be integrated into Unified Command to ensure the

---

[166] U.S. Department of Justice, *AG Guidelines* (May 30, 2002), 10.

[167] Title 18, U.S.C. Sections 1951-1968.

[168] U.S. Department of Homeland Security, *National Incident Management System* (Washington, D.C., March 1, 2004).

coordination of FBI efforts with state and local law enforcement activities. The integration of FBI command and control assets does not negate or diminish the responsibility that state and local officials have for directing law enforcement activities at PCSEs.

2. Information Sharing

Different law enforcement agencies working the same crisis events use different information technology (IT) solutions for managing crisis information. The FBI and other law enforcement agencies routinely work around this limitation by exchanging liaison officers between different command posts and operations centers in an attempt to maintain situational awareness. This method of information sharing is dependent upon having the right liaison officers in the right command centers at the right time. Information exchange occurs around specific issues and problems, but there is often no ongoing exchange of "routine" information. The result is that different command centers maintain separate event logs with disparate information. There is no standardized format for exchanging electronic information and there is no common operating picture – a problem that leads to duplication and inefficiency in law enforcement resource allocation.

According to Templar Corporation's W. Ross Ashley, "Effective critical incident response for homeland security requires access to real-time information from many organizations. Command and control, as well as basic situational awareness, are all dependant on quickly communicating a dynamically changing picture to a variety of decision makers."[169] The NIMS specifically addresses the importance of a common operating picture. It states:

> Integrated systems for communication, information management, and intelligence and information sharing allow data to be continuously updated during an incident, providing a common framework that covers the incident's life cycle across jurisdictions and disciplines. A common operating picture helps ensure consistency at all levels of incident management across jurisdictions, as well as between various governmental jurisdictions and private-sector and nongovernmental entities that are engaged.[170]

---

[169] W. Ross Ashley, "Homeland Security: Sharing and Managing Critical Incident Information," *Sensors, and Command, Control, Communications, and Intelligence (C3I) Technologies for Homeland Defense and Law Enforcement II*, Edward M. Carapezza, Ed., Proceedings of SPIE 5071 (2003), 6.

[170] U.S. DHS, *National Incident Management System,* 49.

A common operating picture is especially important during critical incidents and special events. The FBI uses an incident management database called ICON to manage crisis information. ICON is compatible with the FBI's Automated Case System (ACS) and information that is collected and recorded during crisis operations is synchronized and uploaded to ACS so that the FBI maintains only one official system of records. Much of the information collected during special events, particularly politically-charged special events that involve protest activity, may not be collected or recorded in ICON or ACS because of federal privacy legislation. The FBI has an operational need to monitor that activity for planning and situational awareness, however, so a system was developed to track, display, and disseminate incident-related information that does not meet the criteria for inclusion in an FBI database of record.

In May 2004, a tool was developed that allows the FBI and other law enforcement agencies to share investigative and unclassified intelligence information through an IT application that is independent of ICON or ACS. The solution is Internet-based and secure, and it can be accessed by anyone involved in law enforcement or public safety. The Virtual Command Center (VCC) on the Law Enforcement Online (LEO) network provides a mechanism for local, state and federal law enforcement agencies to track, display and disseminate incident and administrative information in almost real time in a secure, accessible, and cost-effective way using the existing secure LEO information-sharing network.

Many information management tools are available and emerging to perform incident command and control. While no single integrated system or network exists for performing this function, programs to set standards and to establish what systems are interoperable would go far toward satisfying responders' needs.[171] LEO is a recognized and accepted mechanism for sharing information and it is compatible with many existing and emerging law enforcement and homeland security communications tools.

In 2002, a Web interface was designed and implemented that provides a seamless bridge between LEO and the Bureau of Justice Assistance's Regional Information

---

171 The National Memorial Institute for the Prevention of Terrorism and the U. S. Department of Homeland Security, *Project Responder: National Technology Plan for Emergency Response to Catastrophic Terrorism,* Thomas M. Garwin, Neal A. Pollard, and Robert V. Tuohy, Eds. (Washington, D.C., April 2004), 72.

Sharing Systems (RISS) network.[172] The RISS program supports federal, state, and local law enforcement efforts to combat criminal activity that extends across jurisdictional boundaries. It provides information sharing, data analysis, investigative support, specialized equipment, technical assistance and training to support investigative and prosecutive efforts that address multi-jurisdictional offenses and conspiracies.[173]

The Department of Homeland Security developed the Joint Regional Information Exchange System (JRIES) to facilitate the exchange of homeland security information between the Homeland Security Operations Center (HSOC) and other homeland security entities. JRIES evolved into the Homeland Security Information Network (HSIN), which is now DHS' primary information sharing network for local, state and federal homeland security professionals. JRIES/HSIN, RISS.net and LEO are complementary programs, and an interface has been built between JRIES and RISS.net that focuses on terrorism.[174] Although the technical piece has not yet been fully developed, the LEO VCC is expected to be fully compatible with HSIN. Once established, this compatibility will allow law enforcement officials to push incident management information (with law enforcement sensitive information redacted) to homeland security officials for situational awareness and potential action.

The VCC is still considered a "work in progress," but it is a powerful tool that serves to improve situational awareness during critical incidents and special events. It is a low-cost, high-impact IT solution that provides a common operating picture for public safety officers and agencies involved in critical law enforcement and homeland security operations.

E. ISSUES AND POLICY CONSIDERATIONS

There are two primary issues that policymakers must consider when considering the use of FBI resources in the policing of PCSEs – First Amendment concerns and Privacy Act concerns.

---

[172] Diane Frank, "Justice Pools Online Resources," *Federal Computer Week* 16, 30, (August 26, 2002), 10.

[173] U.S. Department of Justice, Bureau of Justice Assistance, *Program Brief: Regional Information Sharing Systems Program,* Open-file report, NCJ 192666 (Washington, D.C., April 2002), 3.

[174] U.S. Department of Homeland Security, *Press Release: Homeland Security Information Network to Expand Collaboration, Connectivity for States and Major Cities* (Washington, D.C., February 24, 2004).

1.   First Amendment Concerns

The First Amendment to the United States Constitution guarantees, among other things, freedom of speech, the right of the people peaceably to assemble, and the right to petition the government for a redress of grievances.[175] Aggressively integrating federal law enforcement resources in managing PCSEs may be seen as having a chilling effect on the free exercise of these rights. Law enforcement has the responsibility of balancing the legitimate need to maintain public order with the important interest in protecting First Amendment rights.[176] Effective integration of FBI resources can preserve that balance if those assets work within the existing tools and controls that currently impact federal law enforcement operations.

The U.S. Supreme Court noted in *NAACP v. Claiborne Hardware Co.*, that "the First Amendment does not protect violence" [where] "there is no question that acts of violence occurred."[177] The use of FBI resources should be limited to specifically targeting individuals who engage in violent criminal acts during PCSEs, and they should not be employed to monitor First-Amendment protected activities or in cases where there is a question about whether or not violence is likely to occur.

Additional controls exist that are sufficient to address other First Amendment concerns. The use of FBI assets in policing PCSEs is subject to FBI Headquarters, Department of Justice (DOJ), and Congressional oversight. Federal prosecutions cannot be initiated without the full participation of DOJ and DOJ guidance specifically addresses federal prosecution of violent crimes in aid of racketeering.[178] The guidance directs United States Attorneys to use the racketeering statute selectively based on such factors as the type of defendants involved, the relative ability of the Federal and State authorities to investigate and prosecute, and the apparent involvement of organized crime figures or

---

[175] U.S. Constitution, amend.1.

[176] Daniel L. Schofield, "Controlling Public Protest: First Amendment Implications," *FBI Law Enforcement Bulletin* 63, no. 11 (November 1994), 25-32.

[177] NAACP v. Claiborne Hardware Co., 458 U.S. 916 (1982); cited in Jaime I. Roth, "Reptiles in the Weeds: Civil RICO vs. The First Amendment in the Animal Rights Debate," *University of Miami Law Review* 56, no. 2 (2002), 486.

[178] Title 18 U.S.C. Section 1952.

the lack of effective local investigation because of the interstate features of the crime.[179] Even when such factors are present; however, DOJ cautions that the statute is to be applied "cautiously and in coordination with state and local officials, to avoid jurisdictional conflicts."[180] The proposed state/federal integration strategies are consistent with the guidance provided by DOJ.

Privacy Act concerns. The Privacy Act of 1974 resulted from the abuses of the FBI during the counterintelligence programs (COINTELPROs) of the 1960s and 1970s. The Privacy Act governs the collection, use, or dissemination of records maintained on individuals.[181] The Act has two provisions that are significant to this discussion. Section 552a (e) (1) directs each federal agency to only retain information about individuals in its records that is "relevant and necessary" to an authorized agency mission. Section 552a (e) (7) provides that each agency shall "maintain no record describing how any individual exercises rights guaranteed by the First Amendment unless...pertinent to and within the scope of an authorized law enforcement activity."[182]

The use of FBI resources is only advocated for implementation within the scope of an authorized law enforcement activity. According to the AG Guidelines, information may be collected, retained, and disseminated if it pertains to an open inquiry or investigation; provides the predicate to open a new inquiry or investigation; or is relevant to any other authorized FBI law enforcement function.[183] Employing FBI resources in the management of PCSEs falls within the guidelines because the FBI has the responsibility and jurisdiction for management of special events and investigation of federal crimes – two authorized law enforcement functions.[184]

There are distinct differences between the COINTELPROs of the 1960s and 1970s and the proposed integration of FBI assets into the policing of PCSEs. First, the

---

179 United States Department of Justice, *Resource Book: Handbook on the Comprehensive Crime Control Act of 1984 and Other Criminal Statutes Enacted by the 98th Congress"* (Washington, D.C., December 1984), 100.

180 Ibid.

181 Title 5 U.S.C. Section 552a.

182 Ibid.

183 U.S. Department of Justice, *AG Guidelines*, (May 30, 2002), 23.

184 President Clinton, *PDD-62;* U.S. Department of Justice, *AG Guidelines* (May 30, 2002), 15.

COINTELPROs were instituted in an era when the FBI was not subject to the intense scrutiny it faces today. Second, the COINTELPROs were *covert* programs that supported the "massive surveillance and intelligence apparatus of the Bureau, which had long functioned to identify 'subversive' threats to national security."[185] The Bureau did not seek to react in a measured way to specific criminal activity, it acted "covertly and proactively to hinder targets' capacity to engage in protest activity."[186] The proposed solution to the current problem is to integrate FBI assets *overtly* with other local and state law enforcement officers and to target FBI resources only at those individuals involved in violent criminal activity.

---

[185] David Cunningham, "Understanding State Responses to Left- versus Right-Wing Threats: The FBI's Repression of the New Left and the Ku Klux Klan," *Social Science History* 27, no. 3 (2003), 329.

[186] David Cunningham, "The Patterning of Repression: FBI Counterintelligence and the New Left," *Social Forces* 82, no. 1 (September 2003), 210.

LIST OF REFERENCES

Advisory Panel to Assess Domestic Response Capabilities for Terrorism Involving Weapons of Mass Destruction, Second Annual Report, II. 2000. *Towards a National Strategy for Combating Terrorism* (Washington, D.C., December 15).

Alfano, William. 2005. U.S. Department of State. OSAC Threat Overview, Overseas Security Advisory Council (OSAC) 2006 Security Briefing. U.S. Department of State (Washington, D.C., June 17).

Ashley, W. Ross. 2003. "Homeland Security: Sharing and Managing Critical Incident Information, Sensors, and Command, Control, Communications, and Intelligence (C3I)." *Technologies for Homeland Defense and Law Enforcement II*, Ed. Edward M. Carapezza. Proceedings of SPIE 5071.

Author unknown. *1972 Munich Olympics Tragedy.* http://terrorism.about.com/od/terroristattacksindepth/a/municholympics.htm (Accessed June 11, 2005).

Ballard, Tanya N. 2002. "FBI director unveils plan for agency overhaul." *GOVEXEC.com Daily Briefing* (May 29), http://www.govexec.com/dailyfed/0502/052902tl.htm (Accessed June 11, 2005).

Beutler, Dr. Larry. 2005. *Psychology of Fear Management and Terrorism.* Lecture at the Naval Postgraduate School (Monterey, CA, April 12).

Biddle, Steven D. 2005. *American Grand Strategy After 9/11: An Assessment.* Monograph for the Strategic Studies Institute, U.S. Army War College, ISBN 1-58487-188-1 (Carlisle, Pennsylvania), located at http://www.carlisle.army.mil/ssi/pubs/display.cfm?PubID=603 (Accessed June 6, 2005).

Bolman, L. G., & Deal, T. E. (1997). *Reframing organizations: Artistry, choice, and leadership*, Second Ed. (San Francisco, CA: Jossey-Bass).

Breckenridge, James N. and Philip G. Zimbardo. 2005. *The Media and Disproportionate Fear.* Lecture at the Naval Postgraduate School (Monterey, CA, June 21).

Breckenridge, James N. and Philip G. Zimbardo. 2005. *The Strategy of Terrorism and the Psychology of Mass-mediated Fear.* Unpublished manuscript (Palo Alto, CA).

Bryson, John M. 2004. *Strategic Planning for Public and Nonprofit Organizations*, 3rd Edition. (San Francisco, CA).

Bush, George W. 2001. *Address to Joint Session of Congress.* September 20.

Bush, George W. 2002. *Securing the Homeland, Strengthening the Nation.* (Washington, D.C.).

Bush, George W. 2002. *The National Strategy for Homeland Security* (Washington, D.C.).

Bush, George W. 2003. *Homeland Security Presidential Directive - 7: Critical Infrastructure Identification, Prioritization, and Protection.* (December 17).

Bush, George W. 2003. *Homeland Security Presidential Directive 5. Management of Domestic Incidents.* (February 28).

Bush, George W. 2003. *Homeland Security Presidential Directive 8: National Preparedness.* (Washington, D.C., December 17).

Bush, George W. 2003. *Homeland Security Presidential Directive 5. Management of Domestic Incidents.* (February 28).

Chertoff, Michael. 2005. *Remarks for Secretary Michael Chertoff.* U.S. Department of Homeland Security, George Washington University Homeland Security Policy Institute. (Washington, D.C., March 16) at http://www.dhs.gov/dhspublic/display?theme=44&content=4391 (Accessed June 11, 2005).

Clinton, William Jefferson. 1995. *Presidential Decision Directive 39.* (June 21).

Clinton, William Jefferson. 1998. *Combating Terrorism: Presidential Decision Directive 62.* (May 22).

Cronin, Audrey Kurth. 2004. "Toward an effective grand strategy," in *Attacking Terrorism: Elements of a Grand Strategy.* Cronin, Audrey Kurth and James M. Ludes, Ed. (Washington, D.C.: Georgetown University Press).

Cronin, Blaise. 2005. "Intelligence, Terrorism, and National Security." Annual Review of Information Science and Technology 29., 395-432.

Cunningham, David. 2003. "Understanding State Responses to Left- versus Right-Wing Threats: The FBI's Repression of the New Left and the Ku Klux Klan." *Social Science History* 27, no. 3, 329.

Cunningham, David. 2003. "The Patterning of Repression: FBI Counterintelligence and the New Left." *Social Forces* 82, no. 1, (September), 210.

Decker, Raymond. 2001. "Homeland Security: Key Elements of a Risk Management Approach," testimony before U.S. House of Representatives Committee on Government Reform Subcommittee on National Security, Veterans Affairs and International Relations, *Combating Terrorism: Assessing the Threat of a Biological Weapons Attack*, 107th Cong., 1st Sess., October 12.

108

Decker, Raymond. 2001. *Homeland Security: Key Elements of a Risk Management Approach.* Open-file report: GAO-02-150T (Washington, D.C., October 12).

Domasio, A.R. 1994. *Descartes' error: Emotion, reason, and the human brain.* (New York: Avon).

Dwyer, Timothy. 2005. "Tight Security, Strong Opinions Dominate a Day Full of Divisions." *Washington Post* (January 21).

Fiorell, Joe. 2005. "Critics Slam Both U.S. Parties for Ineffective Antiterror Policies." *Global Security Newswire* at http://www.nti.org/d_newswire/issues/2005_6_2.html#927C7A10 (Accessed June 2).

Frank, Diane. 2002. Justice Pools Online Resources. *Federal Computer Week* 16, 30. (August 26), 10.

Galway, Lionel. 2004. *Quantitative Risk Analysis for Project Management: A Critical Review.* RAND Corporation, Open File Report, WR-112-RC. (Washington, D.C., February).

Goure', Daniel. 2004. "Homeland Security," in *Attacking Terrorism: Elements of a Grand Strategy.* Cronin, Audrey Kurth and James M. Ludes, Eds. (Washington, D.C.: Georgetown University Press).

Hammes, Thomas X. 2005. "Insurgency: Modern Warfare Evolves into a Fourth Generation." *Strategic Forum* 214 (National Defense University: Washington, D.C., January). 7.

Howitt, Arnold M. and Robyn L. Pangi. 2003. *Intergovernmental Challenges of Combating Terrorism in Countering Terrorism: Dimensions of Preparedness.* (Cambridge, MA).

Kean, Thomas H., Chair. 2004. *The 9/11 Commission Report: Final Report of the National Commission on Terrorist Attacks Upon the United States.* (New York: W.W. Norton Co., Ltd,).

Kunreuther, Howard and Robert Meyer, and Christopher Van den Bulte. 2004. *Risk Analysis for Extreme Events: Economic Incentives for Reducing Future Losses.* U.S. Department of Commerce, Open-file Report, NIST GCR 04-871 (Philadelphia, PA, October).

Kuper, Simon. 2005. "Sport and terrorism are now inseparable." *Financial Times* (London, England, July 9/10), W21.

Kunreuther, Howard. 2001. *Risk Analysis and Risk Management in an Uncertain World.* Paper for Distinguished Achievement Award, Society for Risk Analysis Annual Meeting (Seattle, Washington, December 4).

Lewis, Ted G. 2004. *Critical Infrastructure Protection in Homeland Security: Defending a Networked Nation*, Volume 1 (Monterey, CA, 2004). 4.

Massucci, Roberto. 2005. Deputy Director, Italian Ministry of the Interior Law Enforcement Office. *The XX Winter Olympic Games Security System, Overseas Security Advisory Council (OSAC) 2006 Security Briefing*. U.S. Department of State (Washington, D.C., June 17).

Moteff, John. 2004. Congressional Research Service. *Risk Management and Critical Infrastructure Protection: Assessing, Integrating, and Managing Threats, Vulnerabilities, and Consequences*. Open-file Report RL32561. (Washington, D.C., September 2).

Mintzberg, Henry, Bruce Ahlstrand, and Joseph Lampel. 1998. *Strategy Safari: A Guided Tour Through the Wilds of Strategic Management*. (New York, NY: The Free Press).

The National Memorial Institute for the Prevention of Terrorism and the U. S. Department of Homeland Security. 2004. *Project Responder: National Technology Plan for Emergency Response to Catastrophic Terrorism*. Ed. Thomas M. Garwin, Neal A. Pollard, and Robert V. Tuohy. (Washington, D.C., April).

Nesterczuk, George. 2002. "A Successful Start for the Department of Homeland Security Requires Management Flexibility." *The Heritage Foundation, Backgrounder* 1572, July 19.
http://www.heritage.org/Research/HomelandDefense/BG1572.cfm (Accessed June 11, 2005)

Roth, Jaime I. 2002. "Reptiles in the Weeds: Civil RICO vs. The First Amendment in the Animal Rights Debate." *University of Miami Law Review* 56, no. 2, 469.

Scheur, Michael. (Anonymous). 2004. *Imperial Hubris: Why the West is Losing the War on Terror*. (Dulles, Virginia).

Shea, Robert. 2005. Director, DHS Integration Staff. Personal interview by the author. (Washington, D.C., May 6).

Schofield, Daniel L. 1984. "Controlling Public Protest: First Amendment Implications." *FBI Law Enforcement Bulletin* 63, no. 11 (November), 25-32.

Slovic, Paul and Melissa L. Finucane, Ellen Peters, and Donald G. MacGregor. 2002. *Risk as Analysis and Risk as Feelings: Some Thoughts About Affect, Reason, Risk, and Rationality*. Paper presented at the annual meeting of the Society for Risk Analysis (New Orleans, LA, December 10) President Clinton, PDD-62.

Slovic, Paul. 1999. Trust, Emotion, Sex, Politics, and Science: Surveying the Risk-Assessment Battlefield. *Risk Analysis* 19 (4) (Kluwer Academic Publishers: August 1999), 689-701.

Sjoberg, Lennart. 2004. *The Perceived Risk of Terrorism.* SSE/EFI Working Paper Series in Business Administration No. 2002:11 (Stockholm, Sweden, January 16).

Tucker, David. 2004. *Asymmetric Warfare and Homeland Security.* Lecture at Lecture at the Naval Postgraduate School (Monterey, CA, June 17).

United Nations. 1987. *Geneva Declaration on Terrorism.* Paper presented at the United Nations General Assembly (Geneva, Switzerland, May 29).

U.S. Congress. Title 5, U.S. Code, Section 552(a).

U.S. Congress. Title 18, U.S. Code, Section 2332b (f) & (g).

U.S. Congress. U.S. Code of Federal Regulations 0.85 (1).

U.S. Congress. 2002. Homeland Security Act of 2002. Public Law 107-296, 6 United States Code 101, November 25, 2002.

U.S. Congress. Title 18, U.S.C. Section 1951-1968.

U.S. Congress. Title 18, U.S.C. Section 33.

U.S. Congress. Title 18, U.S.C. Section 373.

U.S. Congress. Title 18, U.S.C. Sections 112, 878, 1116, and 1201 (a) (4).

U.S. Congress. Title 18, U.S.C. Sections 231, 2101.

U.S. Constitution, amend.1.

U.S. Department of Defense. 1994. *Department of Defense Directive 2000.15: Support to Special Events.* (Washington, D.C., November 21).

U.S. Department of Homeland Security. 2004. *Buffer Zone Protection Program Workshop.* (Washington, D.C., November).

U.S. Department of Homeland Security. 2005. *Draft Special Events Homeland Security Standard Operating Procedures* (Washington, D.C., March).

U.S. Department of Homeland Security. 2005. *Integrated Federal Support Plan for Major League Baseball 76th All-Star Game July 12, 2005 Detroit, Michigan* (Washington, D.C., June).

U.S. Department of Homeland Security. 2005. *Interim National Preparedness Goal. Homeland Security Presidential Directive 8: National Preparedness.* (Washington, D.C.: March 31).

U.S. Department of Homeland Security. 2004. *National Incident Management System.* (Washington, D.C., March 1).

U.S. Department of Homeland Security. 2005. *National Preparedness Guidance. Homeland Security Presidential Directive 8: National Preparedness.* (Washington, D.C.: April 27).

U.S. Department of Homeland Security. 2005. *National Response Plan.* (Washington, D.C., January 6).

U.S. Department of Homeland Security. 2004. *Press Release: Homeland Security Information Network to Expand Collaboration, Connectivity for States and Major Cities.* (Washington, D.C., February 24).

U.S. Department of Homeland Security. 2005. *Prioritized List of Special Events.* (Washington, D.C., April 8).

U.S. Department of Homeland Security, Office of State and Local Government Coordination and Preparedness. 2005. *Target Capabilities List: Version 1.1.* (Washington, D.C., May 23).

U.S. Department of Justice. 2002. Attorney General Guidelines on General Crimes, Racketeering Enterprise and Terrorism Enterprise Investigations, by John Ashcroft (May 30).

U.S. Department of Justice. 1984. Resource Book: *Handbook on the Comprehensive Crime Control Act of 1984 and Other Criminal Statutes Enacted by the 98th Congress.* (Washington, D.C., December).

U.S. Department of Justice, Bureau of Justice Assistance. 2002. *Program Brief: Regional Information Sharing Systems Program.* Open-file report, NCJ 192666 (Washington, D.C., April).

U.S. Department of Justice, Federal Bureau of Investigation. 1999. Resource Book: *Special Events Management Planning Handbook* (Washington, D.C.).

U.S. Department of Justice, Federal Bureau of Investigation. 2004. *Strategic Plan 2004-2009.* (Washington, D.C.).

U.S. Department of Justice, Office of the Inspector General. 2004. *A Review of the FBI's Handling of Intelligence Information Related to the September 11 Attacks.* (Washington, D.C., November).

U.S. Government Accountability Office. 2001. *Homeland Security: Key Elements of a Risk Management Approach.* Statement of Raymond J. Decker, Director, Defense Capabilities and Management. Open-file Report, GAO-02-150T. (Washington, D.C., October 12).

U.S. Government Accountability Office. 2002. *National Preparedness: Integration of Federal, State, Local, and Private Sector Efforts is Critical to an Effective National Strategy for Homeland Security.* Statement of Randall A. Yim, Managing Director, National Preparedness. Open-file Report, GAO-02-621T. (Washington, D.C.).

U.S. Government Accountability Office. 2004. *Combating Terrorism: Evaluation of Selected Characteristics in National Strategies Related to Terrorism.* Open-file report, GAO-04-408T. (Washington, D.C., February).

U.S. Government Accountability Office. 2005. *Olympic Security: U.S. Support to Athens Games Provides Lessons for Future Olympics.* Open-File Report GAO-05-547. (Washington, D.C., May).

U.S. Government Accountability Office. Homeland Security: *A Risk Management Approach Can Guide Preparedness Efforts.* Statement of Raymond J. Decker, Director, Defense Capabilities and Management. Open-file Report, GAO-02-208T. (Washington, D.C., October 31, 2001), 8.

U.S. Supreme Court. *NAACP v. Claiborne Hardware Co.*, 458 U.S. 916 (1982).

Weissman, Robert. 2000. "Puppets, Protestors and Police: April 16 Mobilization Builds Momentum against the IMF and World Bank," *Multinational Monitor* 21, no. 5 (May), 24-29, at http://www.proquest.com/ (Accessed May 24, 2004).

Wikipedia. 2005. The Free Encyclopedia, at http://en.wikipedia.org/wiki/Objective_analysis (Accessed June 18, 2005).

Wikipedia. 2005. The Free Encyclopedia, at http://en.wikipedia.org/wiki/Subjective_analysis (Accessed June 18, 2005).

Woo, Dr. Gordon. 2003. "The Evolution of Terrorism Risk Modeling". Submitted for the *Journal of Reinsurance.* (London, England, April 22).

Yarger, H. Richard. 1997. "Towards a Theory of Strategy: Art Lykke and the Army War College Strategy Model." Cited in Goure'

www.ingramcontent.com/pod-product-compliance
Lightning Source LLC
Chambersburg PA
CBHW052001280526
45793CB00005B/809